Meeting the Needs
of Your Most Able Pupils:
MATHEMATICS

Other titles in the series

Meeting the Needs of Your Most Able Pupils: Art
Kim Earle
1 84312 331 2
978 1 84312 331 6

Meeting the Needs of Your Most Able Pupils: Design and Technology
Louise T. Davies
1 84312 330 4
978 1 84312 330 9

Meeting the Needs of Your Most Able Pupils: Geography
Jane Ferretti
1 84312 335 5
978 1 84312 335 4

Meeting the Needs of Your Most Able Pupils: History
Steven Barnes
1 84312 287 1
978 1 84312 287 6

Meeting the Needs of Your Most Able Pupils: Music
Jonathan Savage
1 84312 347 9
978 1 84312 347 7

Meeting the Needs of Your Most Able Pupils: Physical Education and Sport
David Morley and Richard Bailey
1 84312 334 7
978 1 84312 334 7

Meeting the Needs

of Your Most Able Pupils:

MATHEMATICS

Lynne McClure and Jennifer Piggott

Routledge
Taylor & Francis Group

LONDON AND NEW YORK

First published 2007 by
Routledge
2 Park Square, Milton Park, Abingdon, Oxon OX14 4RN

Simultaneously published in the USA and Canada by
Routledge
270 Madison Ave, New York, NY 10016

Routledge is an imprint of Taylor & Francis, an informa business

British Library Cataloguing in Publication data
A catalogue record for this book is available from the British Library

Library of Congress Cataloging in Publication Data
A catalog record has been requested

ISBN 13: 978 1 84312 328 6 (pbk)
ISBN 13: 978 0 203 93538 5 (ebk)
ISBN 10: 1 84312 328 2 (pbk)
ISBN 10: 0 203 93538 1 (ebk)

Series production editors: Sarah Fish and Andrew Welsh
Typeset by Servis Filmsetting Ltd, Manchester
Printed and bound in Great Britain
by Bell & Bain Ltd, Glasgow

Contents

Foreword

Reasonable people adapt themselves to the world; unreasonable ones persist in trying to adapt the world to themselves. Therefore all progress depends on unreasonable people.

(adapted from George Bernard Shaw, *Man and Superman*)

Great talents are the most lovely and often the most dangerous fruits on the tree of humanity. They hang upon the most slender twigs that are easily snapped off.

(Carl Jung in *Psychological Reflections*)

There is a plethora of research papers and books in mathematics education, and a huge collection of resource and support books for teachers. In amongst all these publications there are a few robust and stable insights. One of these is that expectation (of the learners, of their teachers, and of their parents or guardians) is a dominant force in learners' performance. Another is that when you find some way of working which is effective for a particular group of learners (low attaining, unmotivated, high attaining, displaying gifts and talents), it is also effective with learners who do not obviously fit into that group. Another is that labelling people reinforces behaviour patterns associated with those expectations, and hence the expectations themselves, whereas labelling behaviour enables learners to transcend that way of acting and move on.

Nowhere are these insights more evident than when supporting and challenging learners who display quick thinking and appreciation of mathematical structure. Drawing on their practical experience, the authors of this book not only make a case for, but show how to formulate policies which, if carried through, will support and foster thinking by all children in a school, not just the 'more able'.

One of the principal forces for educational reform worldwide, and certainly in the UK, has been a desire to do more, more effectively, for learners displaying interest in and talent for mathematics. Like all learners, they respond to and thrive on appropriate challenge in a supportive community and in an atmosphere that promotes curiosity, enquiry, and persistence. The challenge to schools is to provide such an atmosphere and to promote the emergence of sub-communities within the school culture. This leads to one of the many tensions and topics for debate in meeting the opportunities afforded by learners displaying mathematical ability: do you select, identify, and then construct special provision for some, or do you build up a community which encourages and challenges all who choose to join in? The first could be described as 'targeting', and is both interventionist and controlling, while the second could be described as 'slipstreaming' and is respectful and empowering. This book provides solid and practical advice for pursuing practical difficulties and challenges of both approaches.

As Shaw suggests, learners who create the most disturbance are sometimes the ones we need to foster most strongly, and as Jung observes, learners displaying extreme talents may be the most psychologically and socially delicate. Whatever the forces operating in young people's lives, school offers an opportunity to enter and experience a special world of intellectual and social challenge, through being in the presence of teachers who themselves have access to that world.

The key to effective mathematics teaching lies in the subtle messages riding on the back of social interactions and expressions of expectations. The socio-mathematical norms of the classroom, also described as mathematical ethos or atmosphere, can have a big impact on learners, as can the nature and style of the questions asked and the tasks proposed. Being in the presence of teachers who not only appreciate mathematics, but actually think about mathematics themselves, contributes to an ambience within which sensitive and reflective ways of working with learners can sustain and promote mathematical thinking. This book provides the kind of support and information that school managers and teachers need in order to be awake to the issues and to make the best possible provision for all their learners, displaying whatever abilities currently.

JOHN MASON
Professor of Mathematics Education, Open University
Senior Research Fellow, Oxford University
May 2007

Acknowledgements

This book is written for the many teachers and children we have worked with, especially our own daughters, Kate, Biddy, Franki, Alice and Roxane, and also our husbands, Roger and Brian, for their patience and support.

Contributors to the series

The authors

Lynne McClure is an independent consultant in the field of mathematics education and G&T. She works with teachers and students in schools all over the UK and abroad as well as Warwick, Cambridge, Oxford Brookes and Edinburgh Universities. Lynne edits several maths and education journals.

Jennifer Piggott is a lecturer in mathematics enrichment and communication technology at Cambridge University. She is Director of the NRICH mathematics project and is part of the eastern region coordination team for the NCETM (National Centre for Excellence in the Teaching of Mathematics). Jennifer is an experienced mathematics and ICT teacher.

Series editor

Gwen Goodhew's many and varied roles within the field of gifted and talented education have included school G&T coordinator, director of Wirral Able Children Centre, Knowsley Excellence in Cities (EiC) G&T coordinator, member of the DfES G&T Advisory Group, teacher trainer and consultant. She has written and edited numerous reports and articles on the subject and co-authored *Providing for Able Children* with Linda Evans.

Other authors

Art

Kim Earle is a former secondary head of art and design and is currently an able pupils and arts consultant for St Helens. She has been a member of DfES steering groups, is an Artsmark validator, a subject editor for G&TWISE and a practising designer jeweller and enameller.

Design and Technology

During the writing of the book **Louise T. Davies** was a part-time subject adviser for design and technology at the QCA (Qualifications and Curriculum Authority), and part of the KS3 National Strategy team for the D&T programme. She has authored over 40 D&T books and award-winning multimedia resources. She is currently deputy chief executive of the Design and Technology Association.

Geography

Jane Ferretti is a lecturer in education at the University of Sheffield working in initial teacher training. Until 2003 she was head of geography at King Edward VII School, Sheffield, a large 11–18 comprehensive, and was also involved in gifted and talented initiatives at the school and with the local authority. Jane has co-authored a number of A level geography textbooks and a GCSE revision book and is one of the editors of *Wideworld* magazine. She is a member of the Geographical Association and a contributor to their journals *Teaching Geography* and *Geography*.

History

Steven Barnes is a former head of history at a secondary school and Secondary Strategy consultant for the School Improvement Service in Lincolnshire. He has written history exemplifications for Assessment for Learning for the Secondary National Strategy. He is now an assistant head with responsibility for teaching and learning for a school in Lincolnshire.

Music

Jonathan Savage is a senior lecturer in music education at the Institute of Education, Manchester Metropolitan University. Until 2001 he was head of music at Debenham High School, an 11–16 comprehensive school in Suffolk. He is a co-author of a new resource introducing computer game sound design to the Key Stage 3 curriculum (www.sound2game.net) and managing director of UCan.tv (www.ucan.tv), a company specialising in the production of educational software and hardware. When not doing all of this, he is busy parenting four very musically talented children!

Physical Education and Sport

David Morley has taught physical education in a number of secondary schools. He is currently senior lecturer in physical education at Leeds Metropolitan University and the director of the national DfES-funded 'Development in PE' project which is part of the Gifted and Talented strand of the PE, School Sport and Club Links (PESSCL) project. He is also a member of the team responsible for developing resources for national Multi-skill Clubs and is the founder and director of the Carnegie Regional Multi-skill Camp held at Leeds Met Carnegie.

Richard Bailey is professor of pedagogy at Roehampton University, having previously worked at Reading and Leeds Metropolitan University, and at Canterbury Christ Church University where he was director of the Centre for Physical Education Research. He is a well-known author and speaker on physical education, sport and education.

Online content on the Routledge website

The online material accompanying this book may be used by the purchasing individual/organisation only. The files may be amended to suit particular situations, or individual learning needs, and printed out for use by the purchaser. The material can be accessed at www.routledge.com/education/fultonresources.asp

01   Institutional quality standards in gifted and talented education
02   Basic audit form
03   Detailed audit form
04   Departmental monitoring and evaluation guidelines
05   Outline form to support action planning
06   Mathematical ability
07   Key review questions
08   Likes and dislikes
09   Pick's Theorem
10   Nine-pin triangles
11   Individual education plan
12   Hints for classroom teachers – dyslexia
13   Teaching pupils with Asperger syndrome
14   Lesson plan: Year 7, mixed ability class
15   Lesson plan: Year 8, top set
16   Problem sheet (Year 8 lesson)
17   Lesson plan: Year 9, top set
18   Lesson plan: Year 11, top set

www.routledge.com/education

Introduction

Who should use this book?

This book is for all those interested in the educational experiences of the most able, and particularly teachers of mathematics working with Key Stage 3 and Key Stage 4 pupils and above. It will be relevant to all those working within the full spectrum of schools from highly selective establishments to comprehensive and other secondary schools as well as some special schools. Its overall objective is to provide a practical resource that heads of department, gifted and talented coordinators, leading teachers for gifted and talented education and classroom teachers can use to develop a coherent approach to provision for their most able pupils.

Why is it needed?

School populations differ greatly and pupils considered very able in one setting may not stand out in another. Nevertheless, whatever the general level of ability within a school, there has been a tendency to plan and provide for the middle range, to modify for those who are struggling and to leave the most able to 'get on with it'. This has meant that many of the most able have:

- not been sufficiently challenged and stimulated

- underachieved

- been unaware of what they might be capable of achieving

- not had high enough ambitions and aspirations

- sometimes become disaffected.

How will this book help teachers?

This book and its accompanying website will, through its combination of practical ideas, materials for photocopying or downloading, and case studies:

- help teachers of mathematics to focus on the top 5–10% of the ability range in their particular school and to find ways of providing for these pupils, both within and beyond the classroom

- equip them with strategies and ideas to support exceptionally able pupils, i.e. those in the top 5% nationally.

What is in this book?

Chapter 1 gives an overview of the current national picture of gifted and talented education, and if you are not in one of the areas of the country where gifted and talented education has had a high profile, this will bring you up to date with what's happening in the rest of the country.

Chapter 2, Policy in Action, describes the content and process of writing a departmental gifted and talented policy and the subsequent action plan. We were undecided whether this chapter should be at the beginning of the book to flag up the following issues, or at the end as a summary. We could therefore imagine you choosing either to read this chapter first as it gives an overview of the detail of the rest of the book or to read it after Chapters 3, 4 and 5.

Chapters 3, 4 and 5 describe in detail crucial aspects of any provision, and you may choose to read these first so that they feed into the policy chapter. Chapter 6 gives some case studies to illuminate many of the points made throughout the book.

Additional material can be found in the appendices and on the accompanying website. There are three types:

(a) support material for professional development that you may choose to use in a departmental meeting

(b) documentation to support some of the processes described in the chapters – for example audit documents

(c) a limited number of resources for classroom use.

Each is referred to in the text.

Terminology

There is much confusion over the terminology of ability. In this book we have tended to use the term 'able'. However in much of the current literature, and in common parlance, the words '**gifted**' and '**talented**' are used and so you will find them here and there especially when we refer to other writing. There is a lengthy discussion of what these terms mean in Chapter 2.

We have used the words 'pupil' and 'student' interchangeably throughout the book; similarly we have not always made a clear distinction between the terms 'head of department' and 'curriculum leader', on the presumption that you will interpret them as it suits your current context.

This book is part of a series dealing with providing challenge for the most able secondary age pupils in a range of subjects. It is likely that some of the others might also contain ideas that would be relevant to teachers of maths, and that the ideas in this book might be shared with colleagues working in other curriculum areas.

CHAPTER 1

Our more able pupils – the national scene

- Making good provision for the most able – what's in it for schools?
- National initiatives since 1997
- *Every Child Matters* and the Children Act 2004
- *Higher Standards, Better Schools for All* – Education White Paper, October 2005
- Self-evaluation and inspection
- Resources for teachers and parents of more able pupils

Today's gifted pupils are tomorrow's social, intellectual, economic and cultural leaders and their development cannot be left to chance.

(Deborah Eyre, director of the National Academy for Gifted and Talented Youth, 2004)

The debate about whether to make special provision for the most able pupils in secondary schools ran its course during the last decade of the twentieth century. Explicit provision to meet their learning needs is now considered neither elitist nor a luxury. From an inclusion angle these pupils must have the same chances as others to develop their potential to the full. We know from international research that focusing on the needs of the most able changes teachers' perceptions of the needs of all their pupils, and there follows a consequential rise in standards. But for teachers who are not convinced by the inclusion or school improvement arguments, there is a much more pragmatic reason for meeting the needs of able pupils. Of course, it is preferable that colleagues share a common willingness to address the needs of the most able, but if they don't, it can at least be pointed out that, quite simply, it is something that all teachers are now required to do, not an optional extra.

All schools should seek to create an atmosphere in which to excel is not only acceptable but desirable.

(*Excellence in Schools* – DfEE, 1997)

> High achievement is determined by 'the school's commitment to inclusion and the steps it takes to ensure that every pupil does as well as possible'.
>
> (*Handbook for Inspecting Secondary Schools* – Ofsted, 2003b)

A few years ago, efforts to raise standards in schools concentrated on getting as many pupils as possible over the Level 5 hurdle at the end of Key Stage 3 and over the 5 A*–C grades hurdle at GCSE. Resources were pumped into borderline pupils and the most able were not, on the whole, considered a cause for concern. The situation has changed dramatically in the last nine years with schools being expected to set targets for A*s and As and to show added value by helping pupils entering the school with high SATs scores to achieve Levels 7 and beyond, if supporting data suggests that that is what is achievable. Early recognition of high potential and the setting of curricular targets are at last addressing the lack of progress demonstrated by many able pupils in Year 7 and more attention is being paid to creating a climate in which learning can flourish. But there is a push for even more support for the most able through the promotion of personalised learning.

> The goal is that five years from now: gifted and talented students progress in line with their ability rather than their age; schools inform parents about tailored provision in an annual school profile; curricula include a gifted and talented dimension and at 14–19 there is more stretch and differentiation at the top end, so no matter what your talent it will be engaged; and the effect of poverty on achievement is reduced, because support for high-ability students from poorer backgrounds enables them to thrive.
>
> (Speech at National Academy for Gifted and Talented Youth – David Miliband, Minister for State for School Standards, May 2004)

It is hoped that this book, with the others in this series, will help to accelerate these changes.

Making good provision for the most able – what's in it for schools?

Schools and/or subject departments often approach provision for the most able pupils with some reluctance because they imagine a lot of extra work for very little reward. In fact, the rewards of providing for these pupils are substantial.

- It can be very stimulating to the subject specialist to explore ways of developing approaches with enthusiastic and able students.

> Taking a serious look at what I should expect from the most able and then at how I should teach them has given my teaching a new lease of life. I feel so sorry for youngsters who were taught by me ten years ago. They must have been bored beyond belief. But then, to be quite honest, so was I.
>
> (Science teacher)

- Offering opportunities to tackle work in a more challenging manner often interests pupils whose abilities have gone unnoticed because they have not been motivated by a bland educational diet.

> Some of the others were invited to an after-school maths club. When I heard what they were doing, it sounded so interesting that I asked the maths teacher if I could go too. She was a bit doubtful at first because I have messed about a lot but she agreed to take me on trial. I'm one of her star pupils now and she reckons I'll easily get an A*. I still find some of the lessons really slow and boring but I don't mess around – well, not too much.
>
> (Year 10 boy)

- When pupils are engaged by the work they are doing motivation, attainment and discipline improve.

> You don't need to be gifted to work out that the work we do is much more interesting and exciting. It's made others want to be like us.
>
> (Comment of a student involved in an extension programme for the most able)

- Schools identified as very good by Ofsted generally have good provision for their most able students.

> If you are willing to deal effectively with the needs of able pupils you will raise the achievement of all pupils.
>
> (Mike Tomlinson, former director of Ofsted)

- The same is true of individual departments in secondary schools. All those considered to be very good have spent time developing a sound working approach that meets the needs of their most able pupils.

> The department creates a positive atmosphere by its organisation, display and the way that students are valued. Learning is generally very good and often excellent throughout the school. The teachers' high expectations permeate the atmosphere and are a significant factor in raising achievement. These expectations are reflected in the curriculum which has depth and students are able and expected to experience difficult problems in all year groups.
>
> (Mathematics Department, Hamstead Hall School, Birmingham; Ofsted 2003)

National initiatives since 1997

In 1997, the new government demonstrated its commitment to gifted and talented education by setting up a Gifted and Talented Advisory Group (GTAG). Since then there has been a wide range of government and government-funded initiatives that have, either directly or indirectly, impacted on our most able pupils and their teachers. Details of some can be found below. Others that relate to mathematics will be found later in this book.

Excellence in Cities

In an attempt to deal with the chronic underachievement of able pupils in inner city areas, Excellence in Cities (EiC) was launched in 1999. This was a very ambitious, well-funded programme with many different strands. In the first place it concentrated on secondary age pupils but work was extended into the primary sector in many areas. Provision for gifted and talented students was one of the strands.

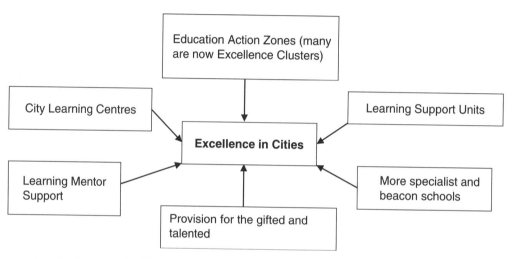

Strands in the Excellence in Cities initiative

EiC schools were expected to:

- develop a whole-school policy for their most able pupils

- appoint a gifted and talented coordinator with sufficient time to fulfil the role

- send the coordinator on a national training programme run by Oxford Brookes University

- identify 5–10% of pupils in each year group as their gifted and talented cohort, the gifted being the academically able and the talented being those with latent or obvious ability in PE, sport, music, art or the performing arts

- provide an appropriate programme of work both within the school day and beyond

- set 'aspirational' targets both for the gifted and talented cohort as a whole and for individual pupils

- work with other schools in a 'cluster' to provide further support for these pupils

- work with other agencies, such as Aimhigher, universities, businesses and private sector schools, to enhance provision and opportunities for these pupils.

Funding changes have meant that schools no longer receive dedicated EiC money through local authorities but the lessons learned from EiC have been influential in developing a national approach to gifted and talented education. **All** schools are now expected to adopt similar strategies to ensure that the needs of their most able students are met.

Excellence Clusters

Although EiC was set up initially in the main urban conurbations, other hot spots of underachievement and poverty were also identified and Excellence Clusters were established. For example, Ellesmere Port, Crewe and Barrow-in-Furness are pockets of deprivation, with major social problems and significant underachievement, in otherwise affluent areas. Excellence Clusters have been established in these three places and measures are being taken to improve provision for the most able pupils. The approach is similar to that used in Excellence in Cities areas.

Aimhigher

Aimhigher is another initiative of the Department for Education and Skills (DfES) working in partnership with the Higher Education Funding Council for England (HEFCE). Its remit is to widen participation in UK higher education, particularly among students from groups that do not have a tradition of going to university, such as some ethnic minorities, the disabled and those from poorer homes. Both higher education institutions and secondary schools have Aimhigher coordinators who work together to identify pupils who would benefit from additional support and to plan a programme of activities. Opportunities are likely to include:

- mentoring, including e-mentoring
- residential summer schools
- visits to different campuses and university departments
- masterclasses
- online information for students and parents
- advice on the wide range of financial and other support available to disadvantaged students.

One national Aimhigher project, Higher Education Gateway, is specifically targeted on gifted and talented students from disadvantaged groups. More information can be found at www.aimhigher.ac.uk.

National Academy for Gifted and Talented Youth (NAGTY)

Government initiatives have not been confined to the most able pupils in deprived areas. In 2002, the National Academy for Gifted and Talented Youth was established at Warwick University. Its brief was to offer support to the most able 5% of the school population and their teachers and parents. It did this in a number of ways:

National Academy for Gifted and Talented Youth		
Student Academy	**Professional Academy**	**Expertise Centre**
• Summer schools including link-ups with CTY in USA. • Outreach courses in a wide range of subjects at universities and other venues across the country. • Online activities – currently maths, classics, ethics, philosophy.	• Continuing professional development for teachers. • A PGCE+ programme for trainee teachers. • Ambassador School Programme to disseminate good practice amongst schools.	• Leading research in gifted and talented education.

NAGTY worked closely with the DfES with the latter setting policy and NAGTY increasingly taking the lead in the practical application of this policy – a policy now known as the English Model, which, as explained on NAGTY's website, is 'rooted in day-to-day classroom provision and enhanced by additional, more advanced opportunities offered both within school and outside of it'. NAGTY ceased operation in August 2007 and was replaced by the Young, Gifted & Talented Programme (see below).

The Young, Gifted & Talented Programme (YG&T)

In December 2006, the UK government announced the creation of a new programme in England, the National Programme for Gifted and Talented Education (NPGATE), to be managed by CfBT Education Trust and now known as the Young, Gifted & Talented Programme (YG&T). Among the changes proposed are:

- a much greater emphasis on school and local level provision.

- the setting-up of Excellence Hubs – HEI-led partnerships to provide non-residential summer schools and a diverse range of outreach provision, including summer activities, weekend events and online and blended learning models. There will be free places for the disadvantaged.

- the appointment of gifted and talented leading teachers – one for each secondary school and each cluster of primary schools.

- a national training programme for gifted and talented leading teachers organised by the national primary and secondary strategies.

Further information about YG&T can be found at www.dfes.gov.uk/ygt or www.cfbt.com.

Gifted and talented summer schools

Education authorities are encouraged to work in partnership with schools to run a number of summer schools (dependent on the size of the authority) for the most able pupils in Years 6–11. It is expected that there will be a particular emphasis on transition and that around 50 hours of tuition will be offered. Some schools and authorities run summer schools for up to ten days whilst others cover a shorter period and have follow-up sessions or even residential weekends later in the school year. Obviously the main aim is to challenge and stimulate these pupils but the DfES also hopes that:

- they will encourage teachers and advisers to adopt innovative teaching approaches

- teachers will continue to monitor these pupils over time

- where Year 6 pupils are involved, it will make secondary teachers aware of what they can achieve and raise their expectations of Year 7 pupils.

More can be found out about these summer schools at www.standards.dfes. gov.uk/giftedandtalented. Funding for them has now been incorporated into the school development grant.

Regional partnerships

When Excellence in Cities (EiC) was first introduced, gifted and talented strand coordinators from different EiC partnerships began to meet up with others in their regions to explore ways of working together so that the task would be more manageable and resources could be pooled. One of the most successful examples of cooperation was the Trans-Pennine Group that started up in the northwest. It began to organise training on a regional basis as well as masterclasses and other activities for some gifted and talented pupils. The success of this and other groups led to the setting-up of nine regional partnerships with initial support from NAGTY and finance from DfES. Each partnership had a steering group composed of representatives from local authorities, higher education institutions, regional organisations concerned with gifted and talented children and NAGTY. Each regional partnership organised professional training; sought to support schools and areas in greatest need; tried to ensure that all 11- to 19-year-olds who fell into the top 5% of the ability range were registered with NAGTY; provided opportunities for practitioner research and arranged challenging activities for pupils. Under the YG&T Programme, nine Excellence Hubs have been created to continue and expand the work of the regional partnerships.

Every Child Matters: *Change for Children* and the Children Act 2004

The likelihood of all children reaching their potential has always been hampered by the fragmented nature of agencies concerned with provision for them. Vital information held by an agency about a child's needs has often been kept back from other agencies, including schools. This has had a particularly negative impact on the disadvantaged, for example, looked-after children. In 2004, 57% of looked-after children left school without even one GCSE or GNVQ and only 6% achieved five or more good GCSEs (see national statistics at www.dfes.gov.uk/rsgateway/). This represents a huge waste of national talent as well as many personal tragedies.

The Children Act 2004 sought to overcome these problems by, amongst other things, requiring:

- local authorities to make arrangements to promote cooperation between agencies to ensure the well-being of all children

- all children's services to bear these five outcomes in mind when planning provision. Children should:

  - be healthy

  - stay safe

  - enjoy and achieve

  - make a positive contribution

  - achieve economic well-being.

There are major implications for schools in seeking to achieve these outcomes for their most able pupils, especially where there is deprivation and/or low aspiration:

- local authorities to appoint a director of children's services to coordinate education and social services

- each local authority to take on the role of corporate parent to promote the educational achievement of looked-after children. This should help to ensure that greater consideration is given to their education when changes in foster placements are being considered

- the setting-up of an integrated inspection regime to look at the totality of provision for children.

More information can be found at www.everychildmatters.gov.uk.

Higher Standards, Better Schools for All (Education White Paper, October 2005)

Although the thrust of this Education White Paper is to improve educational opportunities for all, there is no doubt that some proposals will particularly benefit the most able, especially those that are disadvantaged in some way.

- Pupils receiving free school meals will be able to get **free public transport** to any one of three secondary schools closest to their homes between two and six miles away. At present, such children have very little choice in secondary schooling because their parents cannot afford the fares. This measure will allow them access to schools that might be better able to cater for their particular strengths and needs.

- **The National Register of Gifted and Talented Learners** will record the top 5% of the nation's children, as identified by a wide range of measures, so that they can be tracked and supported throughout their school careers. At first, the focus will be on 11- to 19-year-olds but later identification will start at the age of 4. As a first step, in 2006 all secondary schools were asked to identify gifted and talented students in the school census. In reality, some authorities had already begun this monitoring process but making it a national priority will bring other schools and authorities up to speed.

- In line with new school managerial structures, **'leading teachers' of the gifted and talented** will take the place of gifted and talented coordinators. Training (optionally accredited) will be organised through the national strategies. Leading teachers will work closely with School Improvement Partners and local authority coordinators to implement G&T improvement plans, and undertake much of the work previously undertaken by school coordinators.

- **Additional training** in providing for gifted and talented pupils will be available to all schools.

- **A national programme of non-residential summer schools** will be organised to run alongside gifted and talented summer schools already provided by local authorities and individual schools.

- Secondary schools will be encouraged to make greater use of **grouping by ability** in order to meet the needs of the most able and to use **curriculum flexibility** to allow pupils to take Key Stage 3 tests and GCSE courses early and to mix academic and vocational courses.

- **At advanced level, a new extended project** will allow the most able students to demonstrate high scholastic ability.

- **Extended schools** (see later section).

- **More personalised learning** (see later section).

More information on *Higher Standards, Better Schools for All* can be found at www.dfes.gov.uk/publications/schoolswhitepaper.

Extended schools

In many parts of the country, extended schools are already operating, but it is intended that schools will become much more central in providing a wide range of services to children, parents and the community. The government intends to spend £680 million by 2008 to facilitate these developments. Ideally these services should include:

- all-year childcare from 8.00am to 6.00pm

- referral to a wide range of support services, such as speech therapy, mental health and behaviour support

- exciting activities, including study support and extension/enrichment activities that will motivate the most able

- parenting support, which might include classes on healthy eating, helping children with homework, dealing with challenging behaviour, etc.

- community use of school facilities, especially ICT.

Again, this is an initiative that will benefit all children, especially those whose carers work. However, there are particular benefits for those children whose school performance suffers because they have nowhere to study at home and for those with talents that parents cannot nurture because of limited means.

More information on extended schools can be found at www.teachernet.gov. uk/settingup and www.tda.gov.uk/remodelling/extendedschools.aspx.

Personalised learning

As mentioned earlier in this chapter, a key component of current education reforms is the emphasis on personalised learning – maximising potential by tailoring education to individual needs, strengths and interests. The key features of personalised learning are:

- **Assessment for Learning** – Information from data and the tasks and assessments pupils undertake must be used to feed back suggestions about how work could be improved and what learning they need to do next . . . But the feedback should be a two-way process with pupils also providing information to teachers about factors impeding their learning and approaches that would enhance it. This feedback should inform future lesson planning. For the most able pupils, effective assessment for learning should mean that they move forward with their learning at an appropriate pace and depth, rather than marking time while others catch up.

- **Effective Teaching and Learning Strategies** – It is still the case that many teachers teach only in the way that was most successful for them as learners. There is ample evidence that our most able pupils do not form an homogeneous group and that, in order to bring out their many and varied gifts and talents, we need to adopt a wide range of teaching strategies, making full use of the opportunities provided by ICT. At the same time pupils need to become aware of the learning strategies that are most successful for them, whilst also exploring a broader range of learning approaches.

- **Curriculum Entitlement and Choice** – There are many examples of highly gifted adults whose abilities were masked at school because the curriculum did not appear to be relevant to them. Schools need to take the opportunities afforded by new flexibility in the curriculum, by the specialised diplomas of study being introduced for 14- to 19-year-olds and by partnership with other schools, colleges and businesses to engage their pupils. There are several schools now where more able pupils cover Key Stage 3 in two years. The year that is freed up by this approach can be used in a variety of ways, such as starting GCSE courses early, following an enrichment programme or taking up additional science and language courses. The possibilities are endless if there is desire for change.

- **School Organisation** – Effective personalisation demands a more flexible approach to school organisation. This flexibility might show itself in the way teaching and support staff are deployed, by the way pupils are grouped, by the structure of the school day and by the way in which ICT is used to enable learning to take place beyond the classroom. At least one school is abandoning grouping by age in favour of grouping by ability in the hope that this will provide the necessary challenge for the most able. It remains to be seen how successful this approach is but experimentation and risk-taking is essential if we are to make schooling relevant and exciting for our most able pupils.

- **Partnerships Beyond Schools** – Schools cannot provide adequately for their most able pupils without making full use of the opportunities and expertise offered by other groups within the community, including parents together with family support groups, social and health services, sports clubs and other recreational and business organisations.

The websites www.standards.dfes.gov.uk/personalisedlearning and www.teacher net.gov.uk/publications/ will provide more information on personalised learning, whilst new curriculum opportunities to be offered to 14- to 19-year-olds are described in www.dfes.gov.uk/14-19.

Self-evaluation and inspection

The most able must have as many opportunities for development as other pupils. Poor, unchallenging teaching or an ideology that confuses equality of opportunity with levelling down should not hinder their progress. They should have a fair share of a school's resources both in terms of learning materials and in human resources. The environment for learning should be one in which it is safe to be clever and to excel. These are points that schools should consider when preparing their self-evaluation and school development plans.

There have been dramatic changes in the relationships between schools and local authorities and in the schools' inspection regime since the Children Act 2004. Local authorities are now regarded as commissioners for services for children. One of their tasks is to facilitate the appointment of SIPs, School Improvement Partners, who act as the main conduit between schools and LAs and take part in an 'annual conversation' with their schools when the school's self-evaluation and progress towards targets is discussed.

Self-evaluation is also the cornerstone of the new shorter, more frequent Ofsted inspections, using a SEF (self-evaluation form) as a central point of reference together with the five outcomes for children of *Every Child Matters*. An invaluable tool for schools recognising that they need to do more for their gifted and talented pupils, or simply wanting to assess their current provision, is the institutional quality standards for gifted and talented education (IQS).

Institutional quality standards for gifted and talented education (IQS)

These standards, developed by a partnership of the DfES, NAGTY and other interested groups, are an essential self-evaluation tool for any school focusing on its gifted and talented provision. Under each of five headings, schools look carefully at the level indicators and decide which of the three levels they have achieved:

- **Entry level** – a school making its first steps towards developing a whole-school policy might find that much of its provision falls into this category. Ofsted would rate such provision satisfactory.

- **Developing level** – where there is some effective practice but there is room for development and improvement. This aligns with a good from Ofsted.

- **Exemplary level** – where good practice is exceptional and sustained. Ofsted would rate this excellent.

The five headings show clear links to the personalisation agenda: effective teaching and learning strategies; enabling curriculum entitlement and choice; assessment for learning; school organisation; and strong partnerships beyond school.

Having identified the levels at which they are performing, schools are then able to draw up development plans. A copy of these standards is included in the appendices and more information about them can be found at www2.teachernet.gov.uk/qualitystandards.

Resources for teachers and parents of more able pupils

There is currently an abundance of resources and support agencies for teachers, parents and gifted and talented young people themselves. A few of general interest are included below. Other mathematics examples will be found in later chapters of this book.

World Class Tests

These have been introduced by QCA to allow schools to judge the performance of their most able pupils against national and international standards. Currently tests are available for 9- and 13-year-olds in mathematics and problem solving. Some schools have found that the problem solving tests are effective at identifying able underachievers in maths and science. The website contains sample questions so that teachers, parents and pupils themselves can assess the tests' suitability for particular pupils or groups of pupils, and the tests themselves are also available online. For more information go to www. worldclassarena.org.uk.

National Curriculum Online

This website, administered by QCA, provides general guidance on all aspects of the National Curriculum but also has a substantial section on general and subject-specific issues relating to gifted and talented education, including identification strategies, case studies, management and units of work. Details of the National Curriculum Online can be found at www.nc.uk.net/gt.

G&TWise

G&TWise links to recommended resources for gifted and talented pupils, checked by professionally qualified subject editors, in all subjects and at all key stages and provides up-to-date information for teachers on gifted and talented education. Details can be found at www2.teachernet.gov.uk.

NACE – the National Association for Able Children in Education

NACE is an independent organisation that offers support for teachers and other professionals trying to develop provision for gifted and talented pupils. It gives advice and guidance to teachers and others, runs courses and conferences, provides consultants and keynote speakers.

It has also produced the NACE Challenge Award Framework, which it recommends could be used alongside IQS, as it exemplifies evidence and action planning. While IQS indicates what needs to be improved, the Challenge Award Framework suggests how to effect change. More information can be found at www.nace.co.uk.

National Association for Gifted Children (NAGC)

NAGC is a charity providing support for gifted and talented children and young people and their parents and teachers. It has a regional structure and in some parts of the country there are branch activities for children and parents. NAGC provides: counselling for both young people and their parents; INSET and courses for teachers; publications; activities for 3- to 10-year-olds; and a dedicated area on its website for 11- to 19-year-olds (to which they have exclusive access), called Youth Agency. For further information go to www.nagcbritain.org.uk.

Children of High Intelligence (CHI)

CHI acts on behalf of children whose intelligence puts them above the 98th percentile. It often acts in a support capacity when parents are negotiating appropriate provision with schools and local authorities. For further details visit www.chi-charity.org.uk.

Summary

- Schools must provide suitable challenge and support for their most able pupils.
- Appropriate provision can enhance motivation and improve behaviour.
- Recent legislation to support disadvantaged children should mean that fewer potentially gifted and talented children fall through the net.
- Effective self-evaluation of school provision for gifted and talented pupils and challenging targets are the keys to progress.
- There are many agencies that can help teachers with this work.

Policy in action

- Why have a policy?
- Where to start?
- Issues to bear in mind
- The initial audit
- The main body of the policy
- The action plan
- Where next?

In this chapter we discuss the reasons for having a gifted and talented policy for your department and how you might develop one. However, a policy that has no context is meaningless, so the chapter also discusses the importance of the process of policy formation, its relationship to whole-school policies as well as your general departmental policy, and the resulting implications for development and action plans.

Why have a policy?

Perhaps the first question we need to consider is 'Why should the maths department have a separate gifted and talented policy?' The answer 'because it is a requirement' may be a cynical response and one which drives your initial engagement with the process but of course, there are much better reasons for the activity. The policy is at the core of the provision you offer the able students you teach. It outlines the principles which underpin the actions you take and gives specific guidance within the general context of the whole-school G&T policy. It gives messages to those outside the department and the school, as well as newly appointed members of staff, about what your philosophy is and why, and it reflects not only where you are but also where you want to be – a reflection both of the present state of play and a statement of intent for the future. It is a document that will need regular review if it is to reflect and adapt to changing circumstances.

Although many policies are written because of external pressures, such as access to specific funding opportunities, this is not the best place to start. Ideally, any policy should reflect local needs and local situations and it is these that should be the principal drivers of policy and should affect the detailed implementation. Why? Because the main reason for developing and adopting any policy is to benefit students and you know your students best. You know what the local needs are and what your aims for any development should be. External influences tend to be far too broad-brush and general to have any real 'grounded' value. They may be responsible for initiating the process but should not drive it.

This chapter has been divided into three main sections reflecting the processes of developing and implementing policy; the first gives more detail on the context within which a policy is written and implemented, the second looks at the policy itself, including details of what it should include, and the third considers the action plan and issues of implementation.

Where to start?

The policy should describe:

> how the subject contributes to young people's academic and personal development, and the distinctive qualities and/or context of the subject for gifted and talented learners.
>
> (Subject Guidance: National Curriculum Online)

However, a policy is more than this. It needs to outline the framework in which this will happen. And, once the framework is devised, the real work begins. The policy is only the starting point, and it is what happens in practice that is the most important outcome of the policy and that can be as little or as much as the individuals involved wish it to be. Of course, the aim is to implement the whole of the policy but if in its creation the actions and outcomes envisaged are unrealistic then it has been a pointless exercise. So, not only must the policy and the subsequent action points reflect what is currently happening and what the needs are, they must also take into account what is realistic and feasible. That is why this chapter also discusses action plans and their implementation.

The policy needs to reflect several key aspects:

- national and whole-school policies

- the department's aims and objectives

- the current provision and needs within the department

- the needs of pupils

- staff experience and needs

- curriculum and resource implications

- external support and additional resources

- existing monitoring and evaluation procedures.

Issues to bear in mind

A living document

The first thing to say about any policy is that one of the greatest benefits it can give derives from the process of its creation. Policies written by one member of staff and placed in the departmental library, never to be read again, are not worth the paper they are written on. Any policy should be seen as a dynamic document that is the subject of regular discussion and review because it is only through this process that members of the department can feel ownership and understanding of what any policy contains in fact and in spirit. The process of writing and reviewing any policy depends on staff engagement, both in terms of pooling experiences and expertise, and in identifying need. The consequence of this process is a policy which embeds professional development and is directly linked to practice. This can mean that the period during which the policy is created is generally the most effective, because all those involved in its creation have also been party to its rationale and the, often unstated, 'fine detail'. One would hope that as much of this spirit is visible within the policy as possible. The process can also give staff confidence to discuss any lack of clarity or new situations with colleagues as their ownership of the policy means that any search for clarification or advice is not seen by others as a criticism of their work.

The departmental policy will be unique to the situation and reflect both the department's experience of supporting gifted youngsters and the particular environmental factors at play. The policy needs to be realistic and achievable, reflecting the expertise of the staff within the department and the funding and external support available within the school and from other sources. The policy needs to make explicit its review and evaluation process. Most importantly, it should reflect the needs of the students and staff whom it is designed to support.

The style of the policy

What do you want your policy to look like? How much detail should it contain? In this chapter we outline the content of a potential policy in some detail and, consequently, any policy which addresses all these issues is likely to be extensive and comprehensive. It will represent not only the basic outline of principles and ideas you wish to carry forward but will also give the 'why' as well as the 'what' (the 'how' being reserved for the action plan). However, you or your school may take a view that a policy should be a short document which outlines the major principles and which acts as a reference point for development and action plans. If this is the case then we believe it is very important that the 'why' does not get lost. Supplementary documentation should be kept which illustrates and supports the content of the policy.

The place of the policy

Although this chapter looks specifically at the development of a separate G&T maths policy, some schools prefer to include provision for gifted students within their general teaching and learning policies. In this case it is important to be able to pinpoint those aspects that specifically relate to the G&T agenda as and when needed, and that the discussions and action plans to support provision for mathematically gifted pupils are dealt with specifically.

A framework not a set of rules

Your policy is a framework not a set of rules. The staff who implement the policy and the pupils that the policy is designed to support are all individuals who will act and respond in unique ways. Because of this, you may find it helpful to allow time for discussions based on particular cases and encourage a willingness to consider 'best approaches' in an open environment. It should also be remembered that able pupils are often the best people to explain what their needs are and how these might be met.

All policies have a context

Finally, any policy will need to reflect whole-school policy as well as existing, established, departmental policies. For example, the provision for addressing the needs of the most able within classroom settings may well be different in mixed ability groupings compared to a 'setted' environment. There may also be a school-wide well-established 'withdrawal' mechanism in place which may offer opportunities (if appropriate) which might not be possible to organise within the department. There are also national and regional initiatives that may affect access to funding sources as well as resources.

The subject policy should follow the same framework as the school policy and fit in with its general philosophy. A good policy will come from:

- an audit of current provision and identified needs of pupils and teachers

- an identification of current strengths and what is working well

- staff, including senior management, the school G&T coordinator and the staff within the department

- an identification of what changes need to be made.

Out of the policy should come:

- an action plan which includes clearly defined targets, timescales, responsibilities, resource implications and monitoring and evaluation.

The policy will therefore follow a development, implementation and evaluation cycle such as the one below.

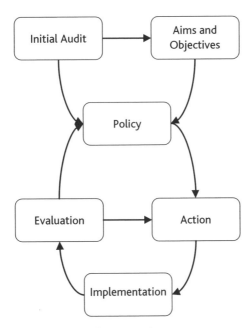

Policy development, implementation and evaluation cycle

The institutional quality standards for gifted and talented provision (see Appendix 1.1) have been developed to support whole-school monitoring. The departmental audit and policy structure in this chapter have been written with these in mind – to offer a departmental outline that can be easily slotted into any school-wide monitoring that may be based on the standards.

The initial audit

It is worth starting the policy creation process by collecting as much information about gifted and talented maths provision generally, as well as the whole-school policy and the department's current position with regard to provision for able pupils. There is probably a great deal of data around that will help you get a picture of what is already going on nationally, regionally, locally and within the school, as well as what you are already doing within the department. Of course, it is important to remember that not all the able pupils in your school are missing out and failing to have their needs met. There are many able pupils who are managing to be highly successful and achieving in line with their potential. This may be because of the nature of the individual, their personal circumstances and/or the provision you are already offering in your department. These successes need to be identified and included in the initial audit so that they can be used to inform the policy creation process, and what happens subsequently.

An audit can be just a list of what's already going on but to be more useful, it should be organised to cover all aspects of the policy. The rest of this section describes some key elements of your initial data collection and audit. Suggested sources for your data are given in the following table.

Sources of data for your audit

Broad area	Evidence from
national and whole-school policies	existing school, LA and national documents, documents such as exemplar policies (whole-school and other departments' policies)
the department's aims and objectives	other departmental policies, e.g. teaching and learning
the current provision and needs within the department	existing data on pupils' attainment level in national tests and other assessment
the needs of pupils	some exemplar case studies, to include pupils who have done well and pupils for whom the process has not been entirely successful. This might include: • how they were identified • what provision curriculum, resource and other adult support was given • how they were assessed before, during and after any intervention • attainment information (above and below norms/expectations in maths or other subjects) • information on transfer and transition • links that were made (with other subjects, external agencies) • pupil commentaries • how the school does or could support pupils with other special educational needs such as dual exceptionality
staff experience and needs	staff views (including G&T coordinator) on current provision and potential future provision based on their experiences, covering a similar list to the above but more generally, and should consider: • communication issues within the department and beyond • support they received or would have benefited from • perceived personal development needs (although these will need reviewing in the light of the policy)
curriculum and resource implications	• classroom observations carried out through a peer-mentoring scheme or specifically to look at provision for able pupils in 'normal' lessons • existing resources and syllabuses • short and medium term plans
external support and additional resources	• views of existing G&T pupils and parents and governors concerning existing provision (you may also be able to use a member of the governing body to take an active part in collecting data for this initial audit – this will inform the governing body of your position and what you are trying to do) • links with learning mentors
existing monitoring and evaluation documents	• external assessment, for example from LA advisers, a recent Ofsted report or a consultancy visit • comparative data from other departments or schools • peer monitoring

You may wish to devise your own audit forms but two examples are given in the appendices. Appendix 2.1 is a blank audit document (like the example below) which can be used by individuals during an initial audit, or for monitoring, but also as the overall audit of provision across the department. Appendix 2.2 contains an overview audit document for the department, based on the Departmental Monitoring and Evaluation Guidelines discussed in the next and following sections. Here is a small example of part of an initial audit done by a teacher; actions were added during discussions in a meeting. The teacher was considering classroom provision and the use of non-teaching staff.

A case study undertaken by a member of the mathematics department as part of an initial audit

Aspect of provision	Commentary	Strengths	Development points	Possible actions
Support	I had a support assistant in the same class as Sophia – they did not work with Sophia though.	Support meant I could give Sophia some special attention sometimes.	Support staff given some training in supporting more able pupils.	Ask SMT about provision and access to training.
	Sophia was interested in doing maths at Oxford – I needed advice on entry and STEP papers.	I was very encouraging and very encouraged.	Possible use of ambassadors scheme from local university. I need to find out about entry requirements.	Discuss specialist support staff and/ or use of other support such as ambassadors from the local university, parents, local business with G&T coordinator. Does LA have links? Look on YG&T and G&T Wise websites for links to support documents.

Once you have completed the initial data collection and audit, the process will have fulfilled two purposes. It will help to inform the policy itself and to establish the starting points for the action plan. The audit can also be very useful when discussing the aims of your gifted provision, as it can stimulate discussion on what matters most to you and your team.

Policy content

Whilst it is useful to look at other maths departments' policies there is also a danger that you reuse others' ideas without engaging with the underpinning principles, or knowing the particular contexts that have affected the choices that were made. Other people's G&T policies are good for offering placeholders and stimulating discussion, but it is the discussion that is important. The purpose of this section is to offer suggestions about what you might include in your policy, not to tell you what you should say. Nothing can fully reflect your particular circumstances like your own policy. Many of the suggestions are written in the form of questions that you might use as a starting point for discussions with colleagues as you formulate your ideas. The structure of this section is based on the departmental monitoring and evaluation guidelines (in Appendix 2.3) which have been developed from the institutional quality standards in gifted and talented education (Appendix 1.1) and which are discussed later in this chapter.

Your policy describes what is important to you and why. Each of the sections below is designed to illustrate some of the key points in more detail. The action plan describes how you are going to do it and so each section finishes with some particular observations which might be useful in formulating the subsequent action plan.

Finally, the creation of your policy may raise many questions to which you do not immediately know the answer. Finding the answers to these questions might form part of your action plan.

What might your policy contain?

At the start of your policy it is useful to include a rationale which might relate it to other policies, a pursuit of excellence and how you see the policy informing practice.

You might also wish to include a statement about what you mean by 'gifted', or 'able', and your use of these terms. Talented is normally applied to learners who have abilities in art and design, music, PE or performing arts such as dance and drama so is not generally applied to ability in mathematics.

Statement of intent

In one or two sentences state what the overarching principles or views on G&T and provision for G&T are. The aim is to give a newcomer an immediate impression of what you are about and to frame the content of the rest of the policy. It is worth trying to write this statement at the start of the policy development but revisit it several times during the process in order to check whether what you are saying reflects the statement or whether the statement needs to be amended in terms of what you are saying.

How the policy relates to the whole-school and other internal policies

Refer to the school's G&T policy – and those aspects of the school's G&T policy that are particularly relevant to you. You might find things at this point that you have difficulty with, for example the school policy talks of acceleration and your department is not in favour of this. The policy needs to state what you hope for but your action plan will need to include a consultation period that addresses the discrepancy between the school's and your philosophy. Often this has happened because the school policy has been written without sufficient communication or you have simply changed your mind, or not considered this as an issue before.

It is here that you might also distinguish between the department's identification strategy (or intended strategy) for the maths cohort, and how it fits with the school's identification procedures. This often raises issues of access to opportunities for some pupils, and flexibility and openness in considering that all pupils are different and may exhibit giftedness in different ways.

Similarly, it is worth looking at a number of other department policies, including related subjects and special needs, to see if there are any synergies or connectivity that can be made. For example, the science department may make specific reference to out-of-school activities that have considerable potential for mathematics and so some work needs to be undertaken to see how the needs of the two subjects might be met most effectively.

Aims

Given your view on G&T, indicated in your statement of intent, what are your aims in addressing that view? They might include statements about:

- to whom the policy applies; by describing the 'most able'? Here you might wish to describe the most able in terms of not merely being about doing well in standard tests or in particular aspects of the subject – or you might wish to include a comment about socio-economic and/or racial or gender balances. You may also like to include an indicative percentage.

- the purposes and processes of identification – this is linked to the opportunities you intend to provide for extending interest, aspiration and achievement.

- inclusion; for example of underachievers and pupils with special needs or those who do not have the advantages of access to positive role models or who lack confidence in their own abilities and potential.

- the aims of the provision you will offer; possibly to develop higher order thinking skills, to encourage a knowledge of what it is to be mathematical and the applicability of the subject and raising aspirations.

- your relationship with interested parties; including the school, parents and carers as well as the individual pupils, and effective use of local and national provision.

- sharing views and opportunities with the community.

- the importance of evaluation and review; in order to encourage pupils and teachers and other members of the community to have ownership of the aims, and to make every effort to meet the needs of your most able pupils.

You might also wish to write an aim which emphasises the importance of staff development.

The main body of the policy

This section discusses the main elements of the policy, listing some ideas and implications for any action plan. Each section has been numbered to match the monitoring and evaluation guidelines in Appendix 2.3. Much of this section has been written in the form of questions that can be used to create the focus of discussions of the policy in meetings.

Identification

1. Introduction

This important feature of the policy is discussed in much greater detail in Chapter 3. However, some indications of what your policy might include in general terms are given below.

- How would you describe the most able and how does this description match school-wide definitions?

- Who is responsible for initial identification? *Class teachers, peers, parents.*

- How will any identification be substantiated? *Subject specialist, outside support.*

- What evidence will be used? *Learning behaviour compared with the peer group, moderation of work by other members of staff, performance in tests, checklists, teacher assessment, liaison with other departments.*

- How does the identification process adopted by the department complement the school policy? *For example, the school policy may require a broad spectrum of achievement but you may want to include pupils performing very highly solely in your subject. A significant discrepancy will be an issue for the action plan.*

- How will you address socio-economic and gender issues?

- What information from primary schools is used to aid identification? How is the department picking up on able pupils identified in their previous schools (this may link to school policy)?

- How is information about able students who move on to sixth forms or other schools or colleges communicated?

- Where and how will records be kept and how often will they be reviewed?

Implications for the action plan – identification

- Lists to support identification are very useful (see Appendix 3.1) but need to be used in combination with other methods.

- Means or comparisons which illustrate the relationship between the school's G&T cohort and the gifted cohort identified with the subject can be useful and help with raising awareness of the needs of pupils who might not be included in targeted whole-school provision. Exemplar case studies can also help shed light on what is intended.

- Cohorts should be regarded as flexible and identification a continuing process not a one-off event. In line with the discussions on classroom practice, whole-class approaches involving problem solving and encouraging aspects of mathematical thinking can give many opportunities for able pupils to shine and be recognised.

- Any identification has to be followed by action.

- Review and evaluation of identification strategies will need to be outlined.

Provision

Under the heading of 'provision', you will need to consider general and individual support outside and inside the classroom. An example of a department (and possibly school) wide decision is whether programmes of whole-class acceleration will be supported and if so, in what circumstances; and, at class level, whether you will support individual or small group programmes of acceleration. In a more general vein, you will need to consider how this provision for able youngsters differs, or if it should differ, from provision offered to all pupils.

Each of the following points will probably have a corresponding entry in the action plan. A number of these points are raised towards the end of the section.

2. Entitlement and choice

- How do syllabuses, schemes of work and lesson plans reflect the needs of the most able students? Will compaction be used and if so how will it be managed? What position is the department taking on withdrawal, acceleration, etc? *For example, the Key Stage 3 Condensed Curriculum Project has been running as a pilot for well over a year. The condensing of the three-year course down into two years is described as having a number of purposes and advantaging a number of audiences, from the least to the most able pupils (DfES and QCA, 2004). This is discussed in greater detail in Chapter 4.*

- Can the department establish any cross-curricular links which can support the particular demands of able youngsters? *For example, in doing some shared project work with the technology department, or supporting the mathematics content of a science project?*

- What long-term, sustainable strategies for provision are available? *For example, if individual pupils are accelerated to work with older peers in order to take GCSE early, can those pupils be supported post-GCSE and how? What choices will be available to them, such as freestanding units, starting an advanced level course early? Is continued acceleration the only long-term strategy available, and what are the advantages and disadvantages for the pupils?*

- What is the role for staff with particular skills and strengths?

- How can individual education plans be used and supported by the implementation of personalised learning pathways?

3. Grouping

There are at least two levels of grouping to consider, the first relates to classes across the department and the second within the classroom. At department level you might wish to discuss mixed ability and setting as two alternative models. It is interesting to note that recent research by Judith Ireson *et al.* (2005) indicated that there is no evidence to suggest that setting, as opposed to mixed ability teaching, benefits pupil performance. Grouping within classrooms is discussed in the classroom provision section. Some questions to consider are:

- What class and departmental grouping strategies can be employed to support the needs of able pupils?

- How will you ensure flexible movement between groups, especially if setting is the preferred strategy?

- Is there the potential for exceptionally able pupils to move between year groups or work independently or in other settings (such as the local sixth form college or sixth form in another school)?

4. In the classroom

The policy needs to articulate a line on the ranges of provision being offered. The following questions might be useful starting points for further discussion.

- How will classroom teaching groups be organised to meet the needs of all pupils including the most able, ensuring challenge and engagement?

- How will the classroom climate support and encourage the most able?

- Will the classroom offer an atmosphere in which the contributions from all pupils are recognised and valued and where enthusiasm for learning is fostered? Are pupils encouraged to be independent, creative problem solvers?

- Will different learning styles be catered for?

- How will able pupils with additional needs be supported? *For example, the use of mentoring for social or skill-based needs and learning support for particular disabilities.*

- What specific learning resources (including ICT) are available for the most able? What types and range of tasks will motivate and engage able pupils, including tasks that require deductive reasoning or application tasks?

- What teaching strategies can be adopted that will support the needs of the most able? *This might include differentiated work, the use of effective questioning and classroom discussion and debate.*

This is discussed in greater detail in the classroom provision chapter.

5. *Learning beyond the classroom*

Chapter 5 looks at possible aspects of provision 'beyond the classroom'. The important things to consider here include:

- What types of provision beyond school are you aware of and how can you find out more?

- What actions can you take to ensure you are aware of the range of provision that might be useful to your pupils?

Implications for the action plan – provision

Many able students make connections and would benefit from having mechanisms for developing links, in cross-curricular projects for instance. Knowing about provision and identification mechanisms used by staff in your department or other departments can also be of great value. How are they providing for able pupils? Is implementation of a system that enables you to develop curriculum and management links within and across departments and nurture more joined-up thinking concerning provision and identification feasible and how can it be achieved? What resources do you need to make such links explicit?

Implications for the action plan – grouping

The organisation of teaching groups will depend on your views of teaching and learning and the approaches that you feel most closely support those views. What actions and resources will be needed to make them happen? For example:

- Will acceleration by class, group or to an older age group be considered and what measures will be taken to support these pupils and to ensure that they continue to make progress in the longer term? Does this have implications for staffing?

- How will you cater for the exceptionally able child? Will you deal with pupils with very special gifts in the subject differently to youngsters who could be described as 'able'?

- Will withdrawal be used? How will pupils who are withdrawn be supported when working back with their peer group?

Mathematics provision needs to consider mathematics not simply as a tool but also as a subject which has value in its own right. The provision should not be one which presents mathematics simply as a toolbox of techniques. It should also encourage pupils in having the experience of being mathematical. How will these views of mathematics relate to provision in lessons?

Personalised learning and concern for the individual does not mean that everyone has to be doing something different. As outlined in the chapter on classroom provision, classroom environments and problems that are accessible to all but can be extended to offer challenges at a range of levels (low threshold, high ceiling tasks) can be used to support personalised learning and assessment for learning. A pamphlet and website on personalised learning is available at www.teachernet.gov.uk/publications/PLbooklet. Personalised learning is important for all pupils but able pupils often have the capabilities to be more self-reflecting and independent, and to support teachers in the identification of their needs and appropriate provision.

Assessment

Clearly assessment needs to relate to targets that are measurable but other rich data, such as attitudes to the subject, attendance and engagement in out-of-school activities, can all add to the picture.

6. Standards

Performance across the department can be used to inform the evaluation of general progress within the school. You will want to reflect on the attainment and achievement of your pupils and this should include qualitative as well as quantitative measures, and use measures of achievement as well as attainment in standard tests. It may well be, for example, that pupils' improved attitudes to, and uptake of, mathematics will result in longer-term benefits for them and for the subject, and result in the number of pupils selecting mathematics-related subjects post-16 increasing.

7. Assessment for learning

Clearly assessment needs to relate to targets that are measurable but opportunities to obtain a picture of the richness of data, including attitudes, attendance and engagement in out-of-school activities, all have something to say about provision. Some aspects of assessment that you should consider include:

- What assessment will be used to enable suitable targets to be set and appropriate progress to be made?

- What measures will be used to assess the academic and attitudinal progress of individuals and of the department as a whole?

- What roles will the students have in their own assessment and planning for future progress? *For example, will you use questionnaires to obtain information such as attitudinal shifts and to find out what extracurricular activities pupils engage in? Will pupils have personal profiles that they can keep up to date or use a reflective diary?*

- How will individual assessments be shared with pupils and how will the pupils be involved in planning their future learning?

Implications for the action plan – assessment

Assessment will play an important role in evaluating individual progress, the progress of particular cohorts of pupils and the progress of the department as a whole when compared to external measures. In devising the action plan you may wish to consider where your priorities need to be and possibly include an action to investigate the range of possible assessment procedures you wish to adopt.

General departmental issues

8. *Ethos and pastoral care*

Some aspects to consider under this heading include:

- How are able pupils viewed in your subject?

- In what ways can you celebrate achievement?

- How can you encourage peer support and mentoring both of and by able pupils?

- How can you support able pupils if they are being bullied or if they feel isolated?

- Where can able pupils go for support?

- How much do you, and should you, welcome parental and other external involvement?

9. *Staff*

This section of the policy should consider the roles of staff, including the member of staff with principal responsibility for gifted pupils.

- What are the roles and responsibilities of the departmental coordinator and all other staff?

- How do these roles link to the school and other subject coordinators?

Some examples of roles and responsibilities are listed below.

Role of the subject G&T coordinator

Responsibilities might include:

- monitoring and identification at transition including pupils arriving from other schools, new intake, etc.
- monitoring identification within school
- ensuring that information on pupils is shared with all staff involved
- monitoring provision for able pupils
- updating colleagues on best practice or new initiatives as they arise
- managing the development of extension and enrichment material
- monitoring, assessment and reviews of pupils' progress
- liaison with other subject coordinators and the school G&T coordinator
- recruitment of help or expertise as required
- liaising with outside agencies
- overseeing the action plan and evaluation and review process, including the regular updating of policy and action plans

- identifying and seeking provision for staff development needs
- reporting to the head of department.

Role of individual staff

- supporting the everyday curriculum needs of individual pupils
- liaising with pastoral and other support personnel within the school when required
- contributing to the development of resources
- monitoring and assessment of individual progress
- identification of personal development needs.

10. Staff development

As observed earlier in this chapter, the production of a policy for gifted or able youngsters is a form of professional development in itself. The audit and discussion of the policy will result in the identification of further development needs and the action plan or any implementation will reveal more.

Some development can be undertaken internally, especially where there is a desire to establish some shared understandings or to produce some core resources, possibly as a mechanism for thinking about underpinning views of learning and consequences for teaching approaches. This might include undertaking a programme of action research. Any programme of professional development should be linked to individual teachers' professional development plans and to department and school developmental priorities.

Finally, the policy will need to be part of any induction programme for new teachers and teaching support staff.

Some questions to answer include:

- What are the mechanisms for sharing good practice? *For example, through case studies or inventories of approaches or the sharing of resources.*

- What are the roles for teaching assistants, learning mentors and other adult helpers?

11. Resources

Resource needs should arise out of the action plan. Within the policy the most important thing to emphasise is that supporting able pupils comes at a cost. You will need to have the resources to support the provision you offer (inside and outside the classroom) and ensure that what is needed can be justified and related to particular actions. Resources will include teaching equipment, staff support materials, staff development and access to external resources and equipment. Every action will have a resource implication. The one that is most usually overlooked is time, and although paying for staff time is a very good use of a budget, it is often not considered in favour of tangible resources. At every point in your policy discussion or action planning you will need to ask the question:

- What are the resource implications of this decision?

12. Transfer and transition

There are two main points of transfer for your pupils – as they arrive in your school and as they leave. However, pupils are experiencing transitions on a daily basis. Key transitions are from key stage to key stage and from year to year and these should be planned to make the move from one phase to another as smooth as possible and to ensure the continuity and sustainability of provision. It is also important to consider the day-to-day transitions pupils experience as they move from one subject lesson to another subject lesson or from topic to topic within your subject.

- What measures will be taken to support able pupils during their transition from primary to secondary school and from secondary school into further or higher education?

- What experiences are your able pupils having in other subject lessons and what might be the impact on their work in the mathematics lesson? *For example, if they are working very independently in their geography lessons, choosing the topics they wish to cover next and receiving specialist one-to-one support for a short time at least once a week and this is always followed by a mathematics lesson, where they are given very limited autonomy, is this an issue?*

- Able pupils do not necessarily excel in every aspect of the subject. What mechanisms are in place that enable them to work differently when they are confident with a topic but consolidate when they need more time?

13. Partnerships

- What is the role of external collaboration and provision in supporting able pupils? *For example, specialist clubs and societies (such as masterclasses), national associations such as YG&T and NAGC, the internet (websites such as NRICH) and outside agencies and experts.*

- How can external activities feed into the school provision and impact on pupils' classroom experiences?

- What links could be available to support transfer to FE and HE courses and career development? *This might include the development of a programme of outside speakers, establishing a mentoring scheme or tapping into other online or regional activities.*

- How can parents/carers be engaged in the provision for gifted pupils?

- How can the department work with local schools and other institutions?

Implications for the action plan – staff development and resources

We have covered a great deal of ground in the above section but we will focus on the two related aspects of the action plan that are often neglected, staff development and resource implications. Needs in these two areas may arise directly from the policy but most often arise naturally out of the action plan. For example, you may wish to offer support for pupils taking YASS modules (www.open.ac.uk/yass) and, as a result, at least one member of staff will need time to learn about them and how the school can support pupils who decide to participate. Any policy which encompasses changing philosophy or more general demands on staff will be accompanied by professional development needs. The policy needs to reflect this and the action plan should outline how such needs will be identified and met.

The policy may wish to identify the types of in-service training activities that will form the core of staff development. In general, one-off days tend not to be effective unless they are part of a managed structure of development and feedback. The answer to the question of what constitutes effective INSET activities will depend very much on individual, departmental and school needs.

You will need to consider long-term as well as short-term development needs, especially if you intend to work on aspects such as teaching styles and schemes of work. What sort of staff development would be needed to support this? How much of this could be achieved through a programme of action research with a focus on particular areas of interest and concern and that can encourage staff discussion based on a common theme?

What materials and resources are required to implement the action plan? Within the classroom, there is a wide range of resources that might help you support your able pupils, including text books and ICT equipment (including software), but it is also important to consider staffing as a resource, including non-teaching staff and mentors. Other resources will be needed to support staff day-to-day activities including reference texts and a computer with internet connection and printer to help access online enrichment or extension materials, and/or to enable the member of staff with responsibility for able pupils to belong to and gain from communicating with online communities.

14. Monitoring and evaluation

In order to monitor and evaluate progress you need to be clear about what you are monitoring and how you will do it. For each aspect you have identified, you will need to decide how you will measure success. The first step is to identify the specific targets you will set. We have suggested some of the sources of data you might use in the first section of this chapter but you will need to decide upon the range of relevant data to use. Will you include pupil attitudes, uptake of mathematics at higher levels? How will you balance the focus on examination and test results and progress on value-added indicators with other forms of data? Are there aspects of what your policy is trying to convey that the measures you have devised do not meet? What other indicators might you use:

- staff views of pupil engagement

- pupils' reflective diaries

- uptake of mathematics related subjects post-16

- questionnaires?

You will also need to decide upon the cycle of evaluation and review of the policy and action plans. What timescales will you use for each aspect?

The action plan

So far we have discussed the initial audit, aims and objectives and the development of the policy, and to some extent monitoring and evaluation procedures as part of the policy. This section focuses on the action plan.

The policy content section above was based on the department monitoring and evaluation guidelines (Appendix 2.3) and made explicit reference to the action plan throughout. There is value in producing a policy simply for the purposes of raising awareness and as a position paper, but this is not really the point. The key to any good policy is the accompanying action plan which details how the policy will be implemented, by whom and over what timescale. The action plan needs careful consideration and targets need to be SMART:

Specific, Measurable, Achievable, Relevant and Time-related.

So your action plan will need to identify:

- specific details of targets that are relevant to your needs

- ways in which you will manage to achieve them. Is it recognisable (measurable)?

- targets that are achievable, that is, they need to take account of where you are now and where you want to be. Are the stepping-stones you identify as targets sufficiently close together that you can manage to reach them?

- the resources required, including money, staffing and access to outside agencies and the senior management team available to make your targets realistic

- a time by which you aim to meet this target

- an evaluation of progress.

An outline form to support action planning is given in Appendix 2.4 and an example of a completed section follows.

Example entry in the action plan

Policy objective	The focus	Targets	Actions	Measurable outcomes	Staff	Resources needed + cost	Completion date	Review date
Identification – parents/carers involved in identification process	Involve parents in process of identification	Implement a system of parental involvement in pupil identification	Find examples of how other schools/ departments involve parents	Examples of other practices collected	JB	Purchase useful books (£95.94)	Mar 1st	
			Decide on a means of involving parents/carers	Methods of involvement agreed at department meeting	JB	Time with G&T coordinator	Apr 1st	
			Write plan which includes procedures	Plan and procedures written for department handbook and agreed by department G&T coordinator and senior management	JB	1 staff day plus agenda item on department meetings	May 1st	
			Write an article for the next school newsletter outlining procedures	Article in June newsletter describing procedures for next year	JB	1 hour secretarial support (£20)	June 1st	
			Implement procedures	System in place	JB		Sept 1st	Dec

Example of an entry in the action plan

Each of the aspects of the policy and issues that arise can be used to identify entries for your action plan. There may also be actions as a result of your initial audit in order to clarify concerns or prepare the ground for actions related to the policy itself. For example, it may not have been possible to find out whether the local university engaged in undergraduate outreach programmes such as ambassadors schemes and you need to investigate this before moving on to establishing a list of key external links.

Having written your action plan, your review and evaluation of progress should be relatively straightforward if you have clear and measurable outcomes. In a sense this review is slightly different to the more general audit of provision that you might wish to carry out once every two years using audit documents such as those supplied in Appendices 2.1 and 2.2. By stopping and looking more broadly at your progress every so often you will not get caught up so much in fine detail that you forget your overarching aims and objectives.

Where next?

This chapter has encouraged you to take a journey from the early stages of thinking about how you support able pupils to implementation and evaluation of actions based firmly on some clearly identified rationale (described in your policy). Through undertaking an initial audit you can assess where you are and this in turn can help you to consider your views on supporting the most able pupils you teach. The policy acts as a framework around which you consider the actions you wish to take in order to meet the goals you feel are important. A time for regular review and reflection is essential – it is unlikely that your views on provision and assessment will change significantly, at least in the medium term, but the ways of representing those views in practice are liable to change as you find out what works and what doesn't and as you learn from experience.

If you and colleagues in other departments in the school are successfully implementing your gifted policy and have evidence to show that you are achieving towards the 'exemplary' end in your provision then you might wish to consider, as a school, applying for a Challenge Award (NACE – www.nace.co.uk).

Finally, you may start to reflect on how special able pupils are and whether what you initially see as provision for the most able actually is valuable to all the pupils you teach.

Identifying able mathematicians

- Some important questions
- What do we mean by 'able'?
- Strategies for identification
- Requirements

The purpose of this chapter is to introduce the key questions to bear in mind when identifying able mathematicians, and to provide some possible answers. A discussion of various identification strategies is followed by a suggested order of operations.

Some important questions

Before we start – nature or nurture?

Is there a 'maths gene'? Simon Baron-Cohen (Baron-Cohen, 2005), working in the psychology department of Cambridge University, is currently undertaking a research project to support his thesis that there is a genetic disposition to mathematical ability, through gathering DNA samples of siblings who all achieve highly (in this case an A at A level). In a separate neuropsychological study, brain images taken whilst the subjects were involved in mathematical reasoning have shown that mathematically talented boys use different parts of their brains to mathematically talented girls, whether they are young teenagers or older college students (Geake, 2003). If we take these findings to their extreme conclusions we might decide that some students will succeed despite, rather than because of, what we offer in school, and others may never be more than barely competent.

Krutetskii, a psychologist who has explored high mathematical ability in great detail, puts up a different argument. He states that whilst certain anatomical and physiological features of the brain and nervous system are present at birth . . . abilities are always the result of development. They are formed and developed in life, during activity, instruction, and training. Abilities are always abilities for a definite kind of activity, they exist only in a person's specific activity. Therefore they can show up only on the basis of an analysis of specific activity. Accordingly, mathematical ability exists only in a mathematical activity and should be manifested in it.

(Krutetskii in Mason *et al.*, 1986, p. 119)

In other words, we can't identify ability unless we offer suitable opportunities. Let's see what those might be.

What do you think?

Let's start by considering a couple of examples.

Beccy, aged 17, Year 13

Beccy achieved an A* in maths GCSE in Year 11. In Year 12 she started the A level syllabus and got an A in Mechanics 1, A in Pure 1 and B in Stats 1. In Year 12 she sat Pure 2, Pure 3 and Stats 2 and got one A and two Bs so her overall grade was a low A. She was very conscientious, made copious notes during class and always completed her homework. She was quite happy to ask for additional explanation or help both in and out of class from her own teacher, other teachers and her friends. When revising she used the textbook rather than her own notes which she found difficult to understand, and worked through the questions she hadn't done from the book before she worked her way through lots of past papers. She enjoyed certain topics such as vectors. She disliked the long context-heavy question in Pure 3 because she couldn't see the point. She was an avid reader but it never occurred to her to follow up anything she had learnt in her maths lessons or explore any topic independently. She got a place at a red-brick university to do a degree which had a considerable maths component.

Ben, aged 12, Year 7

Ben came into the school with a SATs low level 4 in maths and was put into a middle ability set. His handwriting was nearly illegible and he would do anything to avoid recording his work, partly because of his writing difficulty but also because he couldn't see the point when he could do a lot of the thinking in his head. Consequently he had very little in his exercise book. He hated mental arithmetic tests because he was one of the slowest in the class, but he was always accurate and had his own ways of working things out. He often brought in maths puzzles and tricks to show his teacher and she was often surprised at the way he explained them to her. He scored very highly in the annual multiple choice Maths Challenge competition and was invited to take part in the subsequent more difficult rounds, at which he was also very successful.

You may consider both Beccy and Ben to be gifted mathematicians, or perhaps Beccy but not Ben, or Ben but not Beccy, or maybe neither. You and your colleagues' thoughts will be predicated on your definition of giftedness, what you believe about mathematical ability and how it can be detected. In this chapter we look at what others have to say about the issue of thinking mathematically, offer some suggestions for detecting high mathematical ability in the ordinary classroom and link it with classroom provision. We end the chapter by looking at the actions and paperwork to do with identifying able pupils within the maths department, and link it in to the school's policies for able students, and teaching and learning.

Why is it important to identify?

Within schools there are potentially three levels of impact of effective identification – at the student, teacher and institutional level. Students whose individual gifts or talents are correctly identified are likely to receive their educational entitlement – what Winstanley calls 'equality of quality of challenge' (Winstanley, 2005). Those whose individual gifts or talents are missed or remain unfulfilled are likely to become frustrated or worse. For teachers, effective identification helps them to become more effective in their planning, and therefore more sensitive in their appreciation of the needs of *all* their students. At school level, effective identification is a part of high quality provision for the most able, which has been shown to have positive knock-on effects on the quality of teaching and learning generally. Of course we also need to identify and support our most able students nationally – they have an important part to play in the future success of the country.

'But a whole chapter? – we all *know* who are the able/gifted mathematicians in our classes'

Do you believe this about the students in the classes you teach? You may feel very confident that you have been working with your students for such a long time, and know them so well, that you have the whole issue of identifying high ability sorted. Or it may be that you are reading this near the beginning of the school year and you have several groups of students that you have not taught before. How able they are may have been somewhat prejudged by their previous teacher as they are in ability groupings or sets. Whichever of these two situations is applicable, you might want to consider supplementary questions – 'How do I know who is the most able in my classes?' 'What do I look for in what my students do, say, or write that makes me believe they are able mathematicians?' 'What is the evidence upon which I base my conclusions?'

Having reflected on this by yourself you may then wish to compare your answers and thinking with a departmental colleague or perhaps with several colleagues, either informally over coffee, or formally, to start a discussion in a departmental meeting. If your discussion is typical, you will:

- require clarity on the meaning of the words 'able' and/or 'gifted'

- debate the relative importance of formal tests and other assessments

- be curious as to whether your conversation would be similar to one held in the other departments or faculties in the school. Would there be parallels, for example, between your criteria to identify highly able mathematicians and those used by the art department to identify highly able artists?

> ### Support material
>
> Use the *Mathematical ability* document on the website to promote discussion of colleagues' understanding of high ability in general.

It may seem that taking time to have such a discussion is a luxury that can rarely be afforded in the over-full timetable of departmental meetings. But we know from experience that where time is taken to explore such issues, a deeper and shared understanding can be built up which forms a secure foundation on which to build even better provision, not only for the most able in your classes, but for all your students. But let's return to those three bullet points first . . .

What do we mean by 'able'?

Able/highly able/gifted/exceptional . . . ?

One of the first stumbling blocks to productive discussion of the whole issue of relative ability in maths is the terminology and the definitions employed. At best it is oversimplified (top of the class) and at worst involves a circular argument such as 'an able mathematician is one who is more able in maths than most of the class'. In reading the relevant literature it is easy to become confused as different countries associate different meanings with the different words. As described in earlier chapters, in England, within the Excellence in Cities (EiC) project, we have a gifted and talented strategy in which 'gifted' means abilities in the academic subjects such as maths, English and science, 'talented' means abilities in the performing and visual arts and sport, and 'able' is a catch-all, usually referring to students who have abilities in both.

Many people believe this is an unhelpful use of the words gifted and talented, partly because of the confusion between the (various) everyday uses of the words and the rather contrived meaning that the DfES has attached to them. But it does at least serve the purpose of a common usage throughout recent English documentation. At the end of the chapter we will return to this particular English vocabulary and see what effect it has on whom, how and why we identify. In the meantime, in line with the title of this book, we will use the word 'able' and explore what this means in the context of maths.

The advantage of using the term 'able' is that it can be prefaced by comparatives – least, more, most, highly, etc. Trafton (1981) suggests that there are three groups of students who can be described as mathematically able:

- those who learn content well and perform accurately but find it difficult to work at a faster pace or at a deeper level (able)

- those who learn content quickly and can function at a deeper level, and who are capable of solving more complex problems than the average student (more able)

- those who are highly precocious in that they work at the level of students several years older and seem to need little or no formal instruction (exceptionally able).

Actually, of course, there aren't three distinct groups – the nature of mathematics and mathematical ability is such that students could achieve very highly in number and algebra work but be unimpressive in anything to do with geometry, for example. It is therefore probably more acceptable to think of mathematical ability as a continuum, or as a selection of particular characteristics drawn from a wide menu.

So what do we actually mean by being mathematically able, functioning at a deeper level, mathematically precocious? To return to the question posed above – what is it that our students say, do, or write that leads us to believe they are able?

'I just know'

Experienced teachers of any curriculum subject use their wealth of knowledge in many informal and almost subconscious ways to judge ability, and would probably have little problem in identifying the most able in their classes. But asking them to tease out the evidence is sometimes quite difficult and they might well say 'Well I just know'.

Support material

Use the *Mathematical ability* document on the website as a preparatory activity to devising your own checklist of characteristics.

The question has intrigued many researchers and educationalists especially over the last fifty years or so. In possibly the most well-known piece of research in this area, Krutetskii (1976) described the highly able students in his twelve-year study as exhibiting a 'mathematical cast of mind', or of being inquisitive in a mathematical way about the world. He chose to investigate the way his students undertook mathematical problem solving, as he believed that it was in such situations that the spread of ability would be most obvious. From a combination of assumptions, observation and experimentation, he devised a model of mathematical ability which has become an essential part of any discussion about the concept. Although there are other possibly more obvious strategies for identifying talent, the way in which students tackle problems is the easiest to do in a classroom situation and so we will discuss it first.

Strategies for identification

Strategy 1: Problem solving as a vehicle for identification

Krutetskii offered his students a series of mathematical problems. He had hypothesised that the more able students would solve these in ways which were characteristically different to those used by less able students. His characteristics are set out below.

Able pupils can:

- understand the structure of the problem in a way that helps them to know how to begin to solve it

- extract a pattern from a set of examples and generalise it

- generalise approaches to problem solving

- develop chains of reasoning using logic

- leave out steps in an argument

- use mathematical symbols flexibly as an aid to, and as part of, thinking

- think flexibly – change their approach if necessary and switch between different representations or ways of thinking

- start from the answer and work backwards if it seems helpful

- remember generalised relationships, types of problems, and types of solutions.

(Adapted from Kennard, 2001, p. 2)

In 1997 Kennard offered a version of Krutetskii's list to a large group of secondary teachers and found that the majority agreed that highly able students did characteristically behave like that (Kennard, 2001). One extra characteristic was suggested – the ability to grasp new material rapidly. This was not seen as an essential characteristic by Krutetskii but was seen as important by the teachers, many of whom also referred to the pupils' intuitive understanding of the direction of a problem. The idea of intuition had proved interesting to Krutetskii, but he had suggested that it was the combination of a student's prior experiences, and the ability to generalise and to make valid shortcuts, that led to a speedy decision about how to start solving a problem, rather than a characteristic itself. The checklist produced by Krutetskii has been replicated and adapted for different audiences. Guidance in the Key Stage 3 strategy, for example, groups characteristics of able mathematicians under three different headings.

Problem solving

- They are quick to understand and apply knowledge and skills in creative and original ways.

- They often take valid and unexpected short-cuts.

- They show persistence and flexibility when searching for solutions, with a willingness to try different methods.

- They are able to grasp the formal structure of a problem.

- They apply their knowledge to new and unfamiliar contexts.

- They work systematically and accurately.*

Communicating

- They communicate their reasoning and justify their methods.*

- They are fluent with symbolic representation.

- They may see calculations as detail and less important than the problem as a whole.*

Reasoning

- They readily generalise patterns and relationships.

- They reason logically and see flaws in arguments.

- They ask questions that show clear understanding and curiosity.

- They are adept at posing their own questions.

- They make connections between the mathematics they have learnt.

- They are able to reverse mathematical processes.

(DfES, 2005a and 2005b)

Although some pupils may display all of the characteristics above, most will display the majority but not all. Whilst most of the list can be directly mapped to Krutetskii's, those characteristics marked with an asterisk in the Key Stage 3 strategy list are ones that stand outside Krutetskii's model and it is interesting that they are perhaps the ones that are most closely linked to formal recording. Teachers often complain that their students lose marks in written assessments because they do not show their working, or that their working is not presented systematically, or that they make silly inaccuracies. Krutetskii's model would suggest that such assessments do not always allow those with high ability to shine through and in some cases actually mask it. The relationship between assessment and identification is interesting and will be a recurring theme throughout this and subsequent chapters.

What other views are there of mathematical intelligence? Gardner's multiple intelligences (Gardner, 1993) include logical–mathematical intelligence within which, like Krutetskii, he identified fluency in notation, intuition in the direction of a problem, sustaining chains of reasoning and proficiency in the elements of mathematical problem solving. This latter he identified as a) specialising and breaking a problem down into smaller parts; and b) generalising both from sets of information and in the use of problem-solving arguments.

Numerous other writers (Polya, Shoenfeld and Mason, for example) have described, variously but with common themes, what it is to problem solve and/or to think mathematically. The processes they describe fit well with Krutetskii's list of characteristics. We will return to the whole issue of problem solving in greater depth when we discuss classroom provision in Chapter 4, but here it is sufficient to emphasise the link between identification and provision. If we want to identify able students we have to provide them with opportunities to display such characteristics. Problem solving is a good vehicle for this because being a problem solver is what we think it means to be mathematical – so able pupils tend to be good at problem solving. Let's now consider the opportunities afforded through national testing.

Strategy 2: 'Lots of our pupils get good GCSE/A level results so we're doing it right'

We are in a target-driven educational system. Departmental targets feed into school targets which feed into local authority targets and hence national statistics. So who can blame teachers if, having achieved departmental success, they decide that the case for able students is closed? Well, there are three different but equally compelling reasons why the case is definitely not closed.

Firstly, just because able pupils achieve highly doesn't mean they can't be challenged even further. Many students describe maths as boring – either difficult and boring, or easy and boring. Many of the case studies of able mathematicians (NAGTY, 2005) record the sheer tedium of ploughing through the syllabus for GCSE, of operating at a superficial level and doing endless practice papers. These students are just as entitled to an enjoyable and challenging maths experience as anyone else.

Secondly, we know from research (Neiderer *et al.*, 2001, 2003) that tests which require students to 'recall, compute, understand and apply various mathematical operations and concepts' are not accurate in identifying giftedness. Students who scored identical high marks on such standardised multiple choice maths tests differed greatly in their ability to solve mathematical problems. The danger of being drawn into a circular argument is evident. If we define high ability exclusively as high attainment in the sort of national tests we now administer, we are in danger of not identifying mathematical thinkers at all.

This argument is not new. Years ago, Richard Skemp, in what is still regarded as a seminal reading in maths education, described two different types of mathematical understanding, relational and instrumental. He defined relational understanding as the building-up of conceptual structures, whilst instrumental understanding he said was 'rules without reasons' (Skemp, 1971). There are links here to Bloom's taxonomy of educational objectives – the three higher orders of thinking which he describes as analysis, synthesis and evaluation also depend on conceptual structures whereas the lower and middle levels, of knowledge, comprehension and application, can be developed through following those rules

(Bloom, 1956). If we look at the types of assessments we usually employ in mathematics, there is a concentration on testing the lower levels of thinking in Bloom's taxonomy, or instrumental understanding in Skemp's terms.

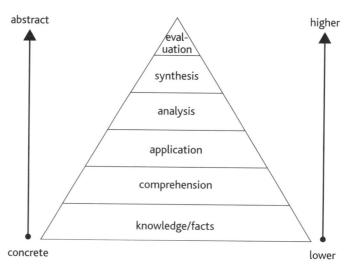

Bloom's taxonomy

More recently Joe Renzulli, director of the Center for Gifted Education & Talent Development in Connecticut, has suggested that there are two broad categories of giftedness (Renzulli, 2005). He calls the first 'Schoolhouse Giftedness'. Students who show great success in test-taking and lesson-learning have high schoolhouse giftedness and are of course readily identified through school assessments. Although his work is not maths based, it is easy to see that Beccy, in our first paragraph, exhibited high schoolhouse giftedness but perhaps not such high 'creative-productive' giftedness, which is the second of Renzulli's categories and which he says is not easily measured through testing.

Thirdly, consider Ben's story at the beginning of the chapter. Here we need to distinguish between high ability and high attainment – Ben undoubtedly thought like a mathematician and yet his attainment in SATs (and subsequent examinations) was unremarkable. High ability and high attainment in national tests don't always go together. Whereas high achievers have obvious formal evidence to support their identification, those for whom there is a mismatch between the two may be missed.

Strategy 3: Other tests

Both problem solving and testing are common methods for identifying mathematical ability. Whilst these are specific to maths, there are some more general strategies that might be considered especially when we are trying to identify underachievers.

The most commonly used intelligence or IQ tests are the Wechsler Intelligence Scale for Children (WISC) and the Stanford-Binet Intelligence Scale (SB). They take 60–90 minutes to complete, and must be administered in this country by an educational psychologist. A student's performance is ranked by comparison of his or her score with those of a large group of peers, the average being a score of 100. A score of 130 on the WISC corresponds approximately to the 98th percentile, meaning that only about 2% of children will achieve a score of 130 or higher. While these tests are good at assessing some skills, they may not reveal all of a student's abilities. Schools or programmes which use only IQ scores as an indicator of ability could underestimate, for example, the abilities of children with English as a second language.

Many writers have suggested that there is more to giftedness than IQ. Renzulli for example lists some historical figures who would not have been included in a gifted programme with a cut-off IQ score of 130: Cervantes, Copernicus, Rembrandt, Bach, Lincoln, Locke and Swift, among others. Renzulli suggests that there are other elements that need to be present to maximise gifted behaviour, such as task commitment and creativity. In his three-ring conception of giftedness, Renzulli argues that above average ability with creativity is not likely to lead to productivity if there is little task commitment. Likewise, above average ability with high task commitment will not lead to new, original or unique concepts or products. We might consider both Beccy and Ben to have two out of the three of Renzulli's elements – in Beccy's case she is missing the creativity element and in Ben's the task commitment.

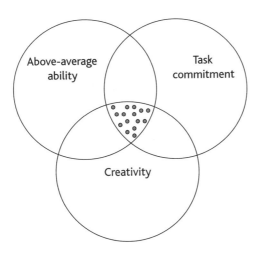

Renzulli's three-ring model

Robert Sternberg's model (Sternberg, 1985) suggests that the *interactions* between the person, the task and their 'cultural fit' will determine success in maximising their gifts. He suggests five criteria for giftedness which include rarity, productivity and value – the excellence the person possesses must be rare relative to peers, and must lead to a product which is valued by his or her society. It is easy to see why these may not be evident in the results of an IQ test.

Many schools in the UK prefer to use the Cognitive Abilities Test (CAT) to assess a range of reasoning skills. The tests look at reasoning with three types of symbols: words, numbers and shapes or figures, i.e. verbal, quantitative and non-verbal reasoning. The non-verbal tests use shapes and figures and are particularly useful when assessing children with poor English language skills, or disaffected pupils who may have failed to achieve in academic work for motivational reasons. CATs are less likely to be affected by poor teaching or poor memory skills as they are not content based. Comparisons between a student's CAT scores and their attainment in school subjects such as English and mathematics can therefore be helpful. These can identify pupils whose reasoning ability is average or above but whose attainment in curriculum-related subjects is low and who may benefit from targeted intervention. Likewise, some students have 'spiky' profiles within a CAT – where one area (such as spatial ability) is high whilst another (such as verbal ability) is quite low. In the classroom situation, the spatial ability may not be evident because it is masked by an inability to comprehend written instructions, and this needs to be investigated further. For more information about CATs you may wish to look at the website (www.nfer-nelson.co.uk/cat/cat_faq.asp). Many schools also use MiDYIS (www.midyisproject.org) and YELLIS (www.yellisproject.org), both of which are designed to measure, as far as possible, ability rather than achievement, fluency rather than knowledge. The basic tests are vocabulary, maths, non-verbal and skills and have been shown to strongly predict subsequent achievement in national tests but can also be useful in identifying students with uneven profiles.

The World Class Tests were devised by QCA (World Class Arena, 2005) specifically 'to identify the most able pupils and to engage and challenge gifted and talented pupils with problems that require them to demonstrate a range of skills and develop their problem-solving skills'. At Brunel University Koshy has found that they are more reliable indicators of high ability than are national tests (Koshy, 2004).

Strategy 4: Nomination

The final strategy for identification is less formal and can involve the students themselves, the peer group, parents and other teachers. However, the reliability of some of these judgements has been shown to be variable. Students' ranking of others' ability correlates highly with that of their teacher whilst student self-perception of high ability has been shown to be closely linked with self-esteem. Working with 10- and 11-year-olds, Neiderer (Neiderer *et al.*, 2003) compared teacher and parental judgments against success on problem solving tasks. She found that non-specialist primary class teachers accurately identified only 50% of those students who scored highly on the tasks, whilst incorrectly identifying as gifted 17% who scored low marks. Parents were more accurate in identifying the high ability of their own offspring (86%) but incorrectly identified low scorers as gifted in 53% of cases. In this research, parents were therefore more likely than primary teachers to identify their own children as mathematically gifted but more likely to identify non-gifted as gifted too.

One might conclude therefore that teacher judgements on ability are not very reliable. The teachers in the study above were primary teachers with a great deal of teaching experience but little specific mathematical pedagogy, and so we might well expect secondary subject specialists' judgements to be more reliable, although to date there is no evidence to support this. But we do know that the more sophisticated teachers become in providing for able students, the more reliable they become at identifying them (Eyre, 1997). Sharing this expertise amongst your department will be important. You could ask colleagues to use one of the checklists as a focus for observing each other's lessons so that teacher nomination can be additionally informed by observation.

A note on underachievers

Later in this book you can read case studies of underachieving able mathematicians. In this chapter we have identified a mismatch of abilities as one possible reason for underachieving in maths – in the extreme this might be, for example, specific learning difficulties such as dyslexia which might prevent access to the full curriculum. There are many 'dually exceptional' (sometimes known as doubly or twice exceptional) students who are identified for their disability rather than their high ability (Eyre and Fitzpatrick, 2000).

There are of course other factors besides a mismatch of abilities, and minimising those might lie within the teachers' remit or might not. Disruptive students who are bored and difficult to teach are undoubtedly a challenge, but boredom can be rectified. The strengths of very able students, such as intense concentration or having diverse interests, may be interpreted as problems (such as stubbornly resisting interruption, or being disorganised) by an unsympathetic teacher. Some students have specific socio-emotional needs which are not met in the ordinary classroom – a professional understanding of these by the teacher might improve such situations but might not fully rectify them.

Support material

Use the *Key review questions* material on the website.

Requirements

So what are you actually required to do?

Working within the school policy on identifying ability, you will be required to identify a group of able maths students across all year groups and record their names. Once the 'cohort' has been identified you will be expected to check that it is representative, as far as possible, of the general school population in terms of gender, ethnicity, socio-economic background, etc., and monitor the membership and achievements of the cohort year on year.

That is the general expectation for all schools. However, within the EiC strategy there are specific percentages and definitions associated with the cohort, which is expected to be 5–10% of the school population. Of this percentage 'gifted' students (including those gifted in maths) make up about two-thirds and the 'talented' the other third. This relative definition means that the cohorts will have very different characteristics in different schools. School A, a highly achieving school, might have an exceptionally able cohort. School B, which is struggling with its number of A–C successes, will have a very different top 5–10% and very few of the students in the school B cohort would come anywhere near getting into the cohort in school A. This relative definition was intended by the DfES to ensure that *all* schools addressed the issue of their most able, but it is not without its problems. Students moving from school to school might find themselves gifted one week and not the next. Colleagues from neighbouring schools working together need to clarify their terms. If your school is not within EiC you can be more creative in your interpretation, although most schools use the EiC guidelines as a blueprint (EiC guidance, 2005).

So who do you place in the cohort? In most schools there are likely to be two overlapping groups. The first will consist of the easily identifiable very able students who not only function well at formal assessments but also meet the characteristics indicated in the lists above. These students would probably be identified as highly able whichever school they attended and are likely to be in the top 5–10% nationally.

The other group comprises those who are the most able in your school. They may not be identified as very able nationally but within your catchment area they are the best. This means that the maths department nominees (together with students from languages, science, English, etc.) will be part of the cohort identified as gifted by the school. Of course, there will be some students who are identified solely on the basis of their mathematical ability, whilst others may be identified in other curriculum areas too. The potential for creative accounting is endless, but your school will have a view on how many all-rounders and how many specialists are to be included.

Within EiC the 'focus is explicitly on ability rather than on attainment or achievement, so underachieving pupils are a priority' (Dracup, 2003). In line with requirements therefore, each department should be actively seeking out those for whom there is a mismatch for whatever reason, and doing something about it. This means that as you monitor the cohort year on year there are likely to be changes. There will be students whose abilities do not develop until later and others who do not continue to meet expectations, and also you and your colleagues will also become more expert over time in recognising less obvious talents.

Officially

The DfES requires schools to keep a record of identified gifted and talented students. This information is entered as part of the PLASC census return. All NAGTY members are expected to be identified too. There are no specific Ofsted requirements other than the all-embracing one of meeting the needs of all students, including the most able.

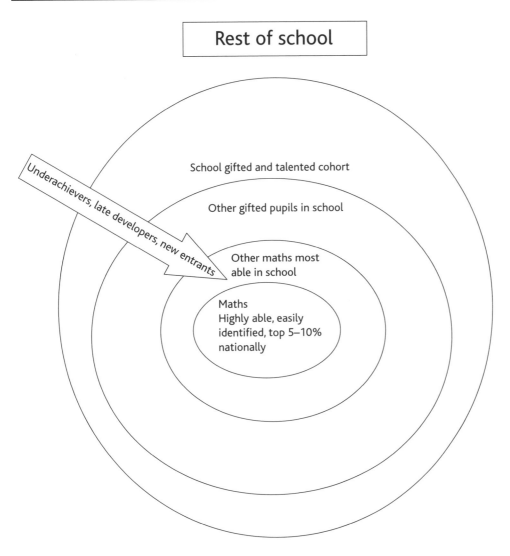

Rest of school

School gifted and talented cohort

Other gifted pupils in school

Other maths most able in school

Maths
Highly able, easily identified, top 5–10% nationally

Underachievers, late developers, new entrants

Cohorts

Institutional quality standards

At entry level, the department is expected to:

- have a system to identify gifted mathematicians in all year groups
- keep a record which meets DfES requirements
- have a representative cohort.

You can read more about the institutional quality standards in Chapter 2.

A suggested order of operations

1. Trawl for the students that everyone agrees are highly able and high achieving. They will be the core of your cohort and any testing, observations or other nominations you do are likely to confirm your judgements.

2. Use one of the many subject specific checklists, or use your own, to confirm your judgements of those you are confident would make the cohort.

3. Suspected underachievers might be the next focus – again using a specific checklist of characteristics, combined with observations, interviews and nominations from parents and peers to obtain a clearer picture of their abilities. Take into account information from previous teachers and previous schools too.

4. Your school may regularly administer CAT or other standardised tests which provide information you can use to identify children with spiky profiles and who have perhaps been overlooked because their disability masks their high mathematical ability.

5. Look at your cohort and check for any mismatch between your nominations and the school profile as a whole. Is there a gender imbalance? Are students for whom English is an additional language adequately represented in your cohort? Or particular ethnic groups? What about students on the special needs register? There may be very good reasons why your cohort is not representative, but asking the questions helps to focus on the maths provision and assumptions you might be making about your students.

6. Communicate the names of students in the cohort to colleagues. There is an expectation that you (or the school G&T coordinator) will also communicate this information to the students themselves and their parents. Bearing in mind that the cohort is likely to change over time, you might want to reflect on how and what exactly you communicate.

7. Monitor the cohort over time and review your assessment and identification strategies – are you using a balanced range or is there still a dependence on test results perhaps? Who is responsible for coordinating and disseminating the information? Are there opportunities for you and your colleagues to discuss some of the deeper issues that will undoubtedly arise?

CHAPTER 4

Classroom provision

- The heart of it – assessment and evaluation
- Down to business – meeting the needs of able mathematicians in the classroom
- Acceleration
- Extension
- Enrichment
- Reflections
- What is a problem and what is problem solving?
- Putting theory into practice – some examples
- Homework
- Action research
- Resources

Introduction

What should we actually be providing for our able students in the classroom? There is of course no single right answer and this chapter is intended to offer you a wide range of possible options together with a discussion about their advantages and disadvantages. The aim is to meet the needs of individuals in a planned, manageable and sustainable way rather than offer an ad hoc, reactive potpourri of activities. We focus on the types of provision possible within the ordinary classroom, because that is where most able students are to be found.

Any provision needs to reflect students' needs and those needs will in turn be based upon where the student is and where he or she is heading in the longer term. In Chapter 3, we talked about the identification of able pupils and stressed the importance of giving opportunities for pupils to show their talents. Any classroom provision therefore has three roles:

- to help identify able youngsters

- to support able youngsters by assessing need

- to develop able youngsters' talents to the full.

These roles can be seen in the DIP/PIP Cycle (Define, Identify, Provide, Identify) based on the DIP cycle of Joan Freeman (2005).

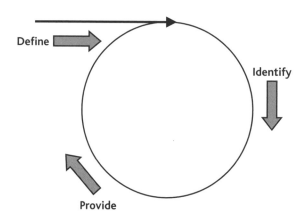

The DIP/PIP cycle – based on the DIP cycle of Joan Freeman

The cycle illustrates the connections between the processes of identification and provision. Starting with your definition of able students you can identify and offer appropriate provision. However, the result of this first cycle is that you will identify pupils who begin to 'emerge' as a result of the provision you offer and your views of what it is to be gifted are modified, so you make additional provision, and so on. One important thing to note is that the original definition has less meaning as your views of the characteristics of able pupils and the type of provision you offer develop.

However, nothing that is being discussed here is just for the benefit of the most able and/or assumes that it is an easy matter to judge what action is best for which student and at what time. We want to ensure that the scope of the provision you offer supports your able pupils in the most effective ways possible. The only word of warning is that a model that focuses on specialised and exceptional provision for youngsters is in danger of being unsustainable. Whatever model(s) of provision you choose it is important to look forward one or two or three years and consider what impact it will have on the students (and not just those at whom the provision is targeted), the teacher and the school then.

The heart of it – assessment and evaluation

How do we know what appropriate provision looks like? The answer is a) by assessing students' learning and b) by evaluating our own teaching, and both should pervade all our practice. The prominence of assessment and evaluation so early in this chapter reflects the importance we believe you should place upon them, because, by keeping them at the core of what you do, you are emphasising that provision is informed by assessment and evaluation, and that it is important that each student's experience is as appropriate and well targeted as possible.

Evaluation of teaching is a continuous activity that takes place on a number of levels. At the informal level, reflective teachers evaluate their teaching almost subconsciously, and at the other extreme, there are formal inspections. There are of course other evaluations – of the resources we use, of our own classroom practice by our peers or formalised self-reflection, of the groupings we choose to work with, or of the structure of our courses – but in this section we will focus on evaluation as it relates to students' learning, and to your department's teaching practices.

Assessment means finding out what students know, understand and can do at any particular point in time. Evaluation is informed by assessment and involves reflecting on how effective our teaching has been in supporting that learning, in order to plan our future actions. So assessment and evaluation are obviously linked in an iterative process (see the assessment evaluation figure later in the chapter).

Assessment before, during and after teaching

What are the major outcomes of classroom-based formative assessment? The example below illustrates the importance of initial assessment and assessment in the course of a lesson, but also the importance of assessing progress at the end of a lesson in order to think about what you will do next. You may wish to reflect on how you might have reacted, and whether you have had a similar experience.

Asha, a Year 9 student, was working in a class that was being introduced to simultaneous equations. The teacher (Mr D) split the class into six groups and gave each group a different word problem that could have been solved using a pair of linear simultaneous equations. However, as Mr D had never taught this topic to them before, the aim was for each group to find solutions which satisfied the conditions using non-standard methods. This would act as a focus for discussion and lead on to an introduction to more formal methods.

Mr D had decided that at the end of the twenty-minute slot he had allocated to each task the groups would stop and discuss their methods and he would pull out key features. There was the potential for some of the groups to have used a substitution or elimination method informally and he would be able to use this experience as a springboard. If not, he would draw on the idea of elegance and efficiency to lead the discussions.

He moved around the class as the groups began to work. If a group had found a solution to their problem, he would ask if there were any more solutions, and whether the group knew that they had all the possible solutions. If a group finished early he was going to give them one of the other problems and ask them to think about how they had tackled the first question and see if they could use what they had learnt to do the second one more quickly. When he arrived at Asha's group (about 5 minutes into the session) the group had already completed their task and had used the method of elimination using algebraic representation for the two variables – this was quite a surprise!

Q. How would you have reacted and what would you have done next?

When discussing the lesson with a colleague later Mr D said he was so surprised he did not know what to do. All his aims for the lesson appeared to have been blown to pieces. He said 'what I should have done is found out what pupils knew already before I started, or at least had something up my sleeve. But I think it would have spoilt the lesson if I had discussed too much to start with as it may have made the groups think there was a particular solution I wanted. After a few seconds of panic, I asked the group to spend five minutes thinking about how they might explain their technique to the rest of the class (I was a bit concerned that Asha may just have dictated the pace and route to the solution and that no one else really understood). After five minutes they would then need to make a choice:

- either they should spend the rest of the time making sure they all understood the explanation, so that if I picked any one from the group they would feel confident to explain what they had done to the rest of the class, or

- they could split up and go and observe (but not talk to) one other group each and see how they were tackling the problems. For the last five minutes they could come back together and see if they could make a connection between what the other groups were doing and what they had done. I would possibly ask them in the second half of the lesson to talk about what they had seen.

In the end I think it went quite well – the group actually spent all the time working out how they might explain it to the rest of the class because, as I sort of expected, Asha had to spend a lot of time going through what they had come up with.'

Mr D then discussed with his colleague what he would need to do in the next lesson to ensure that Asha's group were not twiddling their thumbs whilst he reviewed the findings of the previous day. He would discuss the different methods the groups had adopted and would focus on the technique of elimination adopted by Asha's group. 'I think I will get them to do some examples to practise the technique with Asha acting as mentor and then, when they are ready, I will give them two problems that they can look at when they feel confident to move on; one involving one linear and one quadratic equation, and one with three variables. Some of them may wish to do a few more examples but Asha may like to investigate the other cases.'

Able students very often have prior knowledge of the planned content of our lessons. Clearly what has been described by Mr D is about assessment as a tool that is important for all learners but, in particular, more able pupils are likely to take you by surprise and assessment is a means of helping you to 'be prepared'.

And in between . . .

When pupils enter secondary education they come with information which includes performance in tests and teacher assessment information. This is the first important element in the ongoing process of assessment which you are using in order to ensure that pupils' needs over time are properly catered for.

Actually although the term transition is usually used to mean movement between key stages, it also relates to student transition from one year to another, one topic to another, transition from not knowing to knowing, or from showing little interest or aptitude in a subject to suddenly flowering and so on. One important function of assessment and evaluation is to try to track these transitions in as much detail as possible.

Assessment

Evaluation

Action

Transition

Assessment, evaluation and action should continually support transition

This may seem a daunting task but in every lesson we decide from the evidence in front of us whether pupils have grasped or not grasped an idea, and whether they need support or can move on independently, so this is not rocket science or the impossible dream. As teachers, we monitor transitions all the time. What is being suggested is that, at appropriate moments, some formal noting of that monitoring and evaluation is undertaken so that a picture of a student's progress and journey can be drawn.

Appropriate monitoring and evaluation build on assessment which in turn results in actions, which themselves will need evaluation and so the process continues, and throughout this cycle pupils are in a continuous state of transition.

Assessments can be formal, informal, written or oral; all are equally valid to the teacher. Although some assessments carry much more weight in the wider community it does not mean that they are the most useful forms of assessment in practice. As we read in Chapter 3, scores in statutory tests do give important information about a pupil's performance and understanding but are not sufficient indicators on their own. A pupil who works at very high levels orally may not be able to communicate well in written form. It is the combination of these two pieces of information that tell the teacher that the pupil possibly needs help with written work or with techniques for being successful in high stakes tests, because these will be the key to their moving into higher education. Peer or self-assessment can also be very revealing to you, and useful for the pupils themselves. Reflecting on their own progress and sharing in the setting of new targets gives students a greater responsibility for their own learning and less of a feeling of 'being done to'. Able students in particular dislike being the passive partner in a learning situation.

Naisbett (2003b) lists some of the likes and dislikes of able pupils. These have been included on the website as a possible focus for departmental discussion.

What sort of assessments?

It's therefore important that we offer tasks to assess students across a full range of knowledge, skills and understanding. More of the same questions just test a pupil's understanding of the current topic or their ability to manipulate algorithms. Good mathematicians need to be able to identify what mathematics to use in unusual contexts, so assessments need to draw different aspects of mathematics together by including topics that are not currently under study, or offering tasks which require interpretation in order to be able to solve them. This latter skill is one of the characteristics of able mathematicians, as we discussed in Chapter 3.

We have talked a lot here about the assessment of the pupils but it is also important to evaluate the approaches to teaching and classroom management you are adopting, and the quality of resources you use. To what extent are they achieving the objectives you have for them? Later in the chapter we will discuss styles of working and which resources in particular might prove most useful for able pupils.

Down to business – meeting the needs of able mathematicians in the classroom

There are different ways in which we can adapt the classroom experience for the most able. We can change the way a department or classroom is organised, the questions the teachers ask, or perhaps the order and content of the curriculum. In the literature each model has attracted its supporters and critics, and a great deal of jargon. Before we examine different possibilities, we offer some of the most common definitions below, but with a health warning . . . in the final analysis it's what happens that's important, not whether one can put a name to it!

The basics

Getting through the same work as everyone else but quicker than everyone else – this is usually called **acceleration**.

Exploring mathematics which is not in the national curriculum – this is sometimes called extension, sometimes called enrichment, sometimes called broadening. We're calling it **extension**.

Linking different parts of the maths curriculum or looking at one topic from different perspectives, or asking pupils to 'act like mathematicians' – this is also sometimes called enrichment, sometimes called extension, sometimes called deepening. We're calling it **enrichment**.

More formal definitions

Various descriptions of the following terms are given in the literature but there is no general agreement. The definitions we give below are those we are adopting in this book.

Acceleration

Acceleration is the intentional exposure of pupils to more advanced standard curriculum subject matter with the specific aim of examination on that material in advance of chronological age.

(Piggott, 2006)

Adopting an acceleration model for able pupils should not involve pupils for whom it is not appropriate, for example, accelerating a whole set for the sake of a handful of able pupils.

Extension

Extension is the exposure of pupils to content not normally found in the standard curriculum and which might be considered appropriate to that chronological age or older. Extension can involve giving a context to an application of mathematics or be a focus for learning some new mathematics 'for its own sake'. This could take a number of forms including:

- application of an area of mathematics to different contexts not normally covered within the curriculum (such as some applications to art, astronomy, weather forecasting or computer modelling)

- the opportunity to learn new mathematical content or techniques (such as an introduction to group theory or a particular form of proof). Such content could also include standard curriculum materials met in advance of chronological age.

Enrichment

Enrichment has two key components:

- the content of enrichment is based on opportunities for problem solving through access to problems or problem formulation opportunities which challenge and encourage pupils to make connections within and across content areas

- teaching which encourages problem posing and solving and that builds on discussion and the sharing of ideas. It values difference and pupils as independent, critical thinkers.

Other frequently used terms

Balance and relevance are often used when discussing provision for able students. These terms are not clearly defined and are often used in an inconsistent manner in literature on provision. The following definitions might be useful to help you (and us) to describe resources or classroom practice.

Balance has two interpretations – the need to give a balanced diet of mathematical experience, including opportunities to extend beyond the standard curriculum. It can be argued that even considering this indicates an unbalanced view of the present mathematics curriculum – suggesting that it lacks application to real world contexts or emphasis on problem solving. There is also the sense of balance and harmony in the subject itself and the desire to convey that sense of the subject to the pupils; however, this is not the sense in which this term is usually applied.

Relevance is often reserved for 'real world maths' but we believe this is an abuse of the term. When we talk about relevance we normally mean relevant to the pupil. Much 'real world maths' is used in a contrived way in the classroom and has little or no relevance to the student. Games, interesting mathematical problems, inviting contexts, whether real world or not, can be relevant to the pupil in terms of engagement because of the interest they engender. The intention is to offer mathematics in contexts which engage and 'make sense' to the pupils. Mathematics taught with this philosophy in mind is sometimes known as 'realistic mathematics' and is an approach based largely on the work of Hans Freudenthal.

From exclusive to inclusive

The inclusion agenda is thought by many to be in direct opposition to the agenda for gifted and talented students, but this does not have to be the case. In the following table, we illustrate the range of inclusiveness possible in each of the three models of provision, and in four settings. Each approach (acceleration, extension and enrichment) is discussed below in terms of the first three settings, the fourth (alternative settings) being covered in Chapter 5.

For the acceleration model, each of the three settings is discussed in turn because there are significant differences implicit in the approaches. However, for extension and enrichment, boundaries are less clearly defined and examples of one or two settings are offered to illustrate key points, with references to other settings being made where it seems appropriate.

Let's look at the implications of each of the boxes in the following table. We will consider the advantages and disadvantages for the student, the class as a whole, and the teacher.

Acceleration

Although we have chosen to discuss acceleration first, this should not be taken to mean it is our favourite! Far from it – we believe that acceleration is only appropriate for the exceptionally able child who wishes to be challenged by examinations and has many of the problem solving and mathematical thinking skills, so vital to being mathematical, already to hand. ('Exceptionally able' is not a well-defined phrase and a simple percentage does not describe the complexity of this issue. In addition, even if a pupil is exceptionally able it does not mean that acceleration is the right route for them to take.) For the most able pupils acceleration is frequently the only model of provision on offer and it is not unusual to extend such provision to a much wider cohort than appropriate. Unfortunately many schools use acceleration despite the limited evidence to suggest it is beneficial in the longer term (Boaler *et al.*, 2000; Craven *et al.*, 2000).

We will examine why this is so, and then spend the rest of the chapter looking at other more enjoyable, motivating, challenging and inclusive alternatives.

We believe (and we are not alone) that the number of pupils likely to gain real benefit from opportunities for acceleration is likely to be very small in any school, with at most one or two such pupils in a year group. These pupils are

Models of classroom provision

	Inclusion		Withdrawal	Alternative settings
	Whole-class	Group work	Individualised, within the class or through withdrawal	
Acceleration	Whole class taking early entry to tests or examinations.	Top group in class accelerated. Acceleration is managed per topic (see also group enrichment).	Working alone in class on next level in the programme of study. Might be achieved through use of computer aided learning packages. Working on different areas to the rest of the class.	Moved to another school or class for lessons. They are part of another peer group.
Extension	Whole class working on projects outside standard curriculum content. For example history of mathematics, such as enigma, or mathematical topics such as groups or golden ratio.	Able group of students work on a topic associated with whole class activity, e.g. symmetry in art, whilst rest of class use the topic to consolidate knowledge.	Individual works on a topic in order to feed back into class activity or extend mathematical knowledge. Can link closely to enrichment.	Visits and activities outside the classroom setting including masterclasses, invited speakers, etc.
Enrichment	Problem solving and investigative activities that allow for differentiation (low threshold, high ceiling tasks) where differentiation is possible by outcome.	Top group work on problem associated with whole activity whilst rest of class consolidate. Can link to extension activities. Use of low threshold, high ceiling tasks where 'new' maths can be encountered at the higher levels, e.g. tilted squares. Extension or acceleration through enrichment.	Individual works on associated problem in order to feed back into class activity or as part of personal development in problem solving, including the potential to extend content knowledge.	Masterclasses, mathematics lectures and activities.

those that may be working on higher level topics well in advance of chronological age and who generally show the self-motivation to move on and learn more and need no encouragement to do so (although they like to be encouraged!). Unfortunately, government targets now include success at early entry for GCSE and so teachers can feel pressured into adopting acceleration models.

Acceleration – involving the whole class

We are interpreting this as whole classes of pupils possibly entering Key Stage 3 tests or GCSE early.

Advantages

- Whole-class approaches to acceleration are easy to organise within existing timetable structures.

- Whole-group teaching reduces planning overheads and classroom management issues.

- Students often like the kudos that early entry gives them (Stanley in George *et al.*, 1979).

Disadvantages

- It is often not appropriate for a whole group to be accelerated so some adjustment to numbers may be necessary, or there is a danger of accelerating pupils inappropriately. It is highly unlikely that the standard class size of pupils will contain pupils for all of whom acceleration is appropriate.

- Once a cohort is identified movement into it is very unlikely so pupils who develop later or show potential after the initial period of identification cannot be easily accommodated. Similarly, able students who struggle are at risk of early failure when, if given sufficient time and appropriate support, they might well achieve highly. Is a grade B one year early better than an A* one year later?

- The widest ability range in any class in a school is likely to be in the top set (Sukhnandan and Lee, 1998). If the group is treated as coherent rather than being mixed ability then the needs of the very able, in addition to many of the rest, will still not be met.

Other key issues to consider

- This approach implies that approximately 20% of your cohort (one class out of five) is highly able. The first question to ask yourself is does this seem reasonable?

- What are the pupils who have been accelerated going to do at the end of the accelerated course in the short and, most importantly, in the longer term? Provision needs to plan for years, not a year, ahead.

- There is no evidence to suggest that acceleration benefits all but the smallest minority of pupils and for the rest it is at best neutral.

- How many pupils who take early entry to GCSE in your school go on to take mathematics related subjects in Higher Education? Is this any better than, or worse than, before you introduced a programme of acceleration?

Acceleration – small group

Advantages

- By being prepared to target a small group you are more likely to be finding the most appropriate audience for acceleration.

- Working as a small group there are real opportunities for peer support and sharing.

Disadvantages

- Management of a small, accelerated group in a class is difficult to sustain in the longer term.

- It is hard to keep such a group working in parallel with their peers and this can cause management issues in terms of the amount of teaching time that can be given to students who are working on something different.

Other key issues to consider

A model where acceleration is implemented by topic (for example, work on simultaneous equations, which includes the potential to consider one linear and one quadratic equation for the accelerated group) can work well but needs careful planning. Such approaches would enable some flexibility in the grouping and offer the potential for pupils to step in and out depending on their strengths (although this would make preparation for external examination difficult and becomes rather more like extension, which is discussed later). One could also argue that this becomes no more than a well-planned lesson which takes account of the needs of the most able but with a particular intention to prepare for early entry to external examinations.

Communication and careful record keeping is vital if such an approach is taken in order to ensure full coverage of all aspects of the curriculum.

Acceleration – individualised and alternative setting

Advantages

- Exceptionally able pupils are often highly motivated and can work well with little direct teaching.

- If pupils are taught mathematics through withdrawal, the planning and classroom management can concentrate on the rest of the group.

Disadvantages

- It is easy to forget that being good at passing examinations does not guarantee that the pupil is good at 'being mathematical'.

- These pupils can often become isolated from their peers, especially if models of withdrawal are implemented.

- Additional planning time is needed to prepare for these pupils.

- If the policy is to move very able pupils into the next year group they are unlikely to be working with peers who are their cognitive equals because they in turn have been moved.

- Long-term planning can prove difficult, especially if provision is being offered either through working with an older year group (and this is very difficult to timetable) or entirely off premises (say in a local FE college). How can this model be sustained? What will happen to the pupils when they have completed the courses available?

Other key issues to consider

The possibility of using student volunteers from your local university or remote support by students such as that available through AskNRICH (www.nrich. maths.org) means they can ask questions and discuss mathematics with like-minded youngsters. Be clear about the pupils' longer-term goals. If they wish to take on a mathematics related subject at university what else apart from formal qualifications in mathematics do they need, and should they be devoting more of their time to these needs in order to ensure they can meet their long-term goals?

Consideration should be given to what constitutes these pupils' peer groups and how they can be supported in participating fully and appropriately in those groups.

Extension

Extension activities are often only offered to the most able, but this approach could be embedded in everyday classroom practice allowing all students to benefit from seeing the applications of mathematics to engaging contexts such as those related to 'real world' experiences, games or other topics which simply motivate because of the mathematics they reveal.

The power of extension activities is that, when they are used with the whole class, they allow considerable flexibility. Able pupils can be extended and push ahead whilst others work at their own pace. The different settings (whole class, group and individual) therefore overlap considerably and differ mainly in terms of emphasis. As a result, we have not made a significant distinction between the different approaches to classroom organisation.

Extension – involving the whole class

Planning is undertaken for the whole group and includes material aimed at the most able. Students experience opportunities to see the role, and application, of mathematics in a range of contexts including, where appropriate, beyond the normal curriculum. The aim is to extend the most able within the same or similar contexts to those being introduced to the whole class.

> ### Example
>
> A whole-class theme based on particular art works and focusing on ratio with the potential for some data collection. The question the pupils are asked to answer is 'Do the faces of "beautiful" women have particular proportions and have those proportions changed over time?' and for the most able, 'How often do artists employ the golden ratio? Has it been used anywhere in the design of the school?' Able students are encouraged to investigate properties of the golden ratio, its relationship to the Fibonacci sequence, etc., including research on the internet.

Advantages

- Only one set of planning is necessary.

- There is potential for high levels of engagement because topics can feel highly relevant to the pupils.

- All pupils can feel part of a community sharing in the same mathematics.

- Less able students can use the context to practise and consolidate learned skills whilst able students can use the same situation to extend their mathematical knowledge beyond normal curriculum content.

- There is potential for collaboration and discussion of findings.

- Groups or individuals can develop particular interests and be self-selecting.

- This approach gives flexibility for students to work in different groupings depending on particular mathematical strengths, and thus supports individual needs.

- It enables flexibility of outcome that caters for the range of abilities in a class.

Disadvantages

- Linking outcomes to specific mathematical content may be difficult with extension work as students tend to wander into a particular area of interest or get sidetracked. Careful planning can help with this.

- Planning can be time-consuming in the short term.

- The curriculum structure needs to support this approach by allowing extended time for the work in the long- and medium-term plans.

Extension – small group or individualised work

The first example of group work does not differ significantly from the model of whole-class teaching given above. In this model, the group may be clearly identified at the start of the work and particular objectives identified, though linked to the work of the whole class.

In the second example, the small group is working on a separate topic, which has arisen out of a need in another curriculum area (science). Some discussion between staff has taken place in order to identify this learning opportunity and the need for some additional teaching time has been identified.

Example 1

The class is undertaking work related to a visit to a cotton mill museum. The focus of the work is the loom and involves students investigating weaving patterns, symmetry and proportion (arising from the amounts of each colour yarn needed for the different designs) in order to consolidate recent work on ratio and symmetry. At the same time, a group of more able pupils is using the work on symmetry to introduce them to group theory.

Here the work of the whole group is supplemented by some additional material on a related topic, requiring additional planning and support. The whole class starts with the same theme.

Advantages

- There is potential for collaboration and discussion of findings.

- Contexts can be very stimulating and engaging and able students can pursue an interest in depth and for some time.

- It enables able pupils to work with their peers sharing ideas and expertise.

Disadvantages

- This can be heavy on planning time because you are preparing something separate for the most able. However, resources and activities can be banked within the department for future use.

- Individuals working on extension activities are just as entitled to teacher time as everyone else. Being 'left to get on with it' can be dispiriting and lonely.

Other key issues to consider

The use of adults other than teachers in the classroom can be of great benefit but they need to be clear about learning objectives and expected outcomes. Access to a variety of carefully targeted resources, including online materials, is also very helpful.

Example 2

In a physics lesson, pupils were working on why boats float and the design of tankers. Part of their work involved the creation of a model cargo boat that can carry the most weight for the least surface area. For able students this led into other max-min problems with an exceptionally able pupil starting an early introduction to calculus. The mathematics department were asked if they could support the pupil by introducing calculus.

Advantages

This provision is needs driven and therefore has the potential to be very motivating.

Disadvantages

This requires additional targeted time with the student(s) and further planning time.

Other key issues to consider

Working with older peers as mentors in the classroom or by utilising adults other than teachers can support this approach. It may be necessary to make some time available outside normal lesson time in order to 'kick start' the work.

Enrichment

Like extension, enrichment activities offer the potential of being appropriate for all pupils and can therefore be accommodated within whole-class activities with small groups or individuals working at their own pace, to their own level, with appropriate guidance and support. There does not have to be any explicit separation into whole-class, group and individual work although there may be times when you want to do that.

Enrichment – involving the whole class

The aim of enrichment approaches is that, in classroom settings, able pupils can work as part of the whole group, in smaller groups. A rich task is one which has opportunities for students to work at a wide range of levels of thinking. In Chapter 3 we looked at Bloom's taxonomy and you may wish to refer back to it now. A rich task is one which allows students to think in qualitatively different ways – to operate at Bloom's (1984) lower levels of knowledge, comprehension and application and then the higher levels of synthesis, analysis and evaluation.

The most obvious way to do this is by problem solving. Problem posing and solving are appropriate skills for all to develop and we all do both at some level. Problem solving can be used as a vehicle for learning some new mathematics or developing and consolidating some existing mathematics (often by combining several different mathematical ideas) or as a vehicle for learning how to problem solve. One aspect of problem solving you may be focusing on is the development of convincing arguments related to generalisations which lead in the longer term to more formal proof. Pupils that are more able will enjoy the challenge of convincing their teacher. The two examples below describe contexts in which pupils can be encouraged to give convincing arguments, one geometric and one numeric.

Example 1

Isosceles triangles

Draw some isosceles triangles with an area of 9cm^2 and a vertex at (20,20).

If all the vertices have whole number coordinates, how many is it possible to draw?

Can you explain how you know that you have found them all?

(from www.nrich.maths.org, published Feb 2005)

Example 2

Magic Vs

Use 1 to 5 once only so that the two lines have the same total.

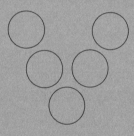

How many different possibilities are there?

Convince me that you have them all.

Advantages

- One task or starting point can be shared by all, and students will progress at different speeds, take up different challenges, and finish in different places.

- All students' problem solving and mathematical thinking skills can be developed and are seen as key components of what it is to be mathematical.

- All pupils learn to see struggle as a normal part of the process and this can in turn support their ability to cope with problem solving beyond and within the classroom, over time.

- Good problem solvers tend to do as well in standard tests but also enjoy the subject more and feel more positive about it.

- Teachers can be highly motivated by students engaging in mathematical discussion and argument.

Disadvantages

- Careful planning is required and confidence to 'let go'.

- If pupils are not used to problem solving approaches they can find this very difficult and it takes time to implement.

- Problem solving appears to take more time (although evidence suggests that the time spent is outweighed by the gains).

Other key issues to consider

Enrichment requires the identification of engaging but challenging contexts and can link to extension. There are many resources available such as the NRICH website, that offer contexts designed specifically for this purpose. But we can also use standard class textbooks – usually the last few questions in an exercise are the most fruitful and lend themselves to being 'opened up'. An example is given later but you might also wish to look at publications such as that written by Prestage and Perks (2001).

In adopting enrichment approaches, you and your colleagues need to be confident enough to give pupils space to explore but with appropriate and timely props (not prompts). It is helpful to have a clear understanding of what the problem or the situation is trying to achieve. For example, if you want your pupils to be more systematic then problems that encourage this need to be identified and objectives shared with the pupils. This approach requires good questioning techniques, open discussion and critical evaluation by pupils. A book such as *Questions and Prompts for Mathematical Thinking* by Anne Watson and John Mason (1998) can be an ideal support.

It is a small step to realise that enrichment offers opportunities for teachers' own professional development in a way that the other models do not. Although paying attention to the types of questions we ask and the opportunities for opening up otherwise closed questions can seem to involve extra work, actually teachers report that over a relatively short period of time these become second nature and happen in all sorts of lessons. Consequently, enrichment can be considered to be of value to all pupils. It also offers potential for long-term gains in terms of attitudes to, and understanding of, what it is to be mathematical through developing an appreciation of mathematics as a discipline.

Reflections

When we use extension and enrichment with the whole class, it is possible to support able youngsters working in groups or individually on similar or related material. Such an approach also supports pupils working with peers, reducing the likelihood of them becoming isolated. There are many examples of very able pupils reflecting on their own maths education and how lonely they found it (NAGTY, 2005). Activities that give flexibility whether they offer opportunities for acceleration or extension or enrichment can be appropriate for all whilst opening up opportunities for the most able – letting the most able fly whilst supporting the least able in developing at their own pace. The most difficult model to implement in this sense is acceleration because of the very clear requirement to 'cover ground'. Renzulli raises the concern that acceleration does not represent a radical departure from an able youngster's usual experiences:

> acceleration is basically a means for quantitative rather than qualitative differentiation.

> (in George *et al.*, 1979, p. 190)

Whole-class teaching in the acceleration model described above, unlike the other two models, is based on treating the class as more or less homogeneous and involves teaching pupils more of the same. In the extension and enrichment models, all pupils can be included in the activities at their own levels. This means whole-class teaching can be inclusive in two senses:

- inclusive in the sense that everyone starts at the same point and can, if they are willing and able, work at the highest level – there are no artificial bars to progression

- inclusive in the sense that the students are in a community of practice working together, albeit at different paces and possibly within a range of learning objectives. Everyone is included in the problem posing and solving process.

The agenda for acceleration is a clear one and is very specifically targeted. This does imply an exclusive view of provision rather than an inclusive one and offers less flexibility in terms of how provision can be met.

The provision through extension and enrichment also opens opportunities for all pupils to develop their higher order thinking skills and not just learn more of the same.

What is a problem and what is problem solving?

Two terms frequently met in school are 'investigation' and 'problem'. In the context of this book, it is worth devoting a few sentences to the connections we see between these terms. The Shorter Oxford Dictionary defines investigation as:

> a systematic inquiry, a careful study of a particular subject

and a problem as:

> an inquiry starting from given conditions to investigate or demonstrate some fact, result, or law.

Investigations in schools often describe open-ended problems which allow pupils to ask their own questions and explore in their own way. In reality, however, we often constrain the freedom to explore because we know there are particular mathematical gems to be found when you follow particular routes.

The purposes and objectives we are trying to meet affect the way in which we present an investigation or a problem. However, we might use the word investigation to describe problems arising from particular mathematical environments that need to be investigated in order to discover the rules that underpin them, for example in investigating Pick's Theorem (see website).

The view of enrichment described above and the role of problems and investigations place a strong emphasis on problem solving. But what do we mean by problem solving and what is a problem?

> A problem is something to which you do not immediately know the answer or a method for finding the answer.
>
> (Piggott and Back, 2004)

A problem to one student therefore may not necessarily be a problem or the same problem to another because:

- they can, or cannot, immediately see how to tackle it, and /or

- they do/don't have the mathematical content skills to solve it, as yet.

The first bullet point distinguishes between those for whom the context is not a problem at all to those for whom it is a problem. The second bullet point begins to draw out the notion of a problem being a different problem for anyone who tackles it.

Amongst the best-known problem solving models was the one suggested by Polya (1957), who described a four-element model. Those four elements (or problem solving heuristics) were:

- understanding the problem

- devising a plan

- carrying out the plan

- looking back.

Polya also described particular techniques that can prove useful within each of these elements. Much of the problem solving literature either develops or reiterates this basic structure and guidance in tackling mathematical problems. Models such as this can help us support pupils in establishing a routine of enquiry and a confidence to step into the unknown and experiencing:

> The joy of confronting a novel situation and trying to make sense of it – the joy of banging your head against a mathematical wall, and then discovering that there may be ways of either going around or over that wall.
>
> (Schoenfeld, 1994, p. 43)

We also need to consider the problem itself, in terms of both its context and its **purpose**.

We suggest the four main purposes for problem solving in the classroom:

- problem solving is a generic skill applicable to other subjects as well as mathematics and is worth doing for its own sake: *teaching for.*

- problem solving can be used as a vehicle for learning mathematical content, whether because it gives purpose to the need for some knowledge or because new knowledge can emerge from it: *teaching through.*

- problem solving should be taught in order for pupils to learn how to problem solve, as the skills cannot be picked up as if by osmosis: *teaching about.*

- problem solving can provide a context or incentive for doing mathematics: *teaching to motivate.*

We think it is important to have these purposes in mind in order to be clear not only about the opportunities problem solving has to open up mathematics to a wider audience but also to help focus on what mathematics you are hoping will come from the process. Different problems will therefore be good for different reasons. Below are some suggested criteria for identifying good problems (although not all the criteria will be appropriate to every problem, as it will depend entirely on its purpose and its audience).

Some criteria for identifying a good problem

The following list can help us when looking for resources that can support problem solving.

Descriptions related to the initial impact of the problem

- uses succinct clear unambiguous language

- draws the solver in

- offers intriguing contexts such that solving them feels worthwhile

- gives opportunities for initial success but has scope to extend and challenge (low threshold, high ceiling problems).

Descriptions related to the experience for the solver

- encourages solvers to think for themselves

- gives the solver a sense of slight unease at first because they are not sure whether the way they are approaching the problem is necessarily going to lead anywhere

- encourages solvers to apply what they know in imaginative ways.

Descriptions related to the problem

- allows for different methods which offer opportunities to identify elegant or efficient solutions

- opens up patterns and connections in mathematics

- leads to generalisations

- reveals underlying principles

- can lead to unexpected results

- requires a solution that calls for a good understanding of process and/or concept and not merely the routine following of a given recipe.

We have so far looked at the advantages and disadvantages of each of the models of provision and made some attempt to describe problem solving in order for us to establish its potential at the core of an extension or enrichment model of provision. This does not exclude the potential to deliver an accelerated programme through problem solving and so, although the focus of much of the rest of the chapter will be on enrichment and extension, the problems have potential to support acceleration models, if that is the route you wish, or have, to take. Having everyone in a class working on an activity or problem, with a small group or an individual aiming to learn new content, and ensuring coverage of the full curriculum content for the acceleration course may be difficult.

Planning for enrichment and extension work is demanding but, in any classroom where all pupils' needs (as individuals) are catered for, planning has the potential to be a nightmare. However, with open tasks (whether open starting points, open middles or open ends) pupils of nearly all abilities can learn something. As discussed in the policy chapter, shared expertise and planning can make an apparently daunting task achievable.

Putting theory into practice – some examples

In this section we first look at a couple of examples that illustrate how you can use existing resources, such as standard textbook questions, and open them up into problem solving activities that have the potential to challenge the most able. This is followed by some detailed case studies of the use of problem solving activities in the classroom.

Closed questions into open tasks

1. The tablecloth (perimeter)

Original problem

A tablecloth is placed over a circular table of diameter 1.6m. If it overhangs by 15cm all the way around – what is the radius of the cloth and how much bias binding will be needed to go around the edge of the tablecloth to hem it (allowing for a 1cm overlap at the ends)?

This could be amended to a problem such as:

Circular tablecloths are made in various sizes starting with a diameter of 1m and increasing in diameter in steps of 10cm. Investigate the amount of bias binding needed for tablecloths of different sizes. Can you explain any patterns you see? Do the same patterns apply to square tablecloths? How about other shapes?

2. Pythagoras' theorem

Original problem

Find the area of an isosceles triangle with these side measurements:

a)   5cm, 5cm, 6cm

b)   13cm, 13cm, 10cm

c)   22cm, 22cm, 13cm.

This could be amended to a problem such as:

Prove that a triangle with sides of length 5, 5 and 6 has the same area as a triangle with sides of length 5, 5 and 8.

Find other pairs of isosceles triangles which are not congruent but have equal areas.

How many isosceles triangles with a base a whole number length have an area of 12 square units?

Using problems as the basis for teaching

Let's take one environment and see how it can be used in a variety of ways.

Example 1

The starting point is a circular pegboard with a centre peg. The number of pegs around the board can vary. (This problem is also available on the website. An interactive version of this environment ('virtual geoboard') can be found on the NRICH website.)

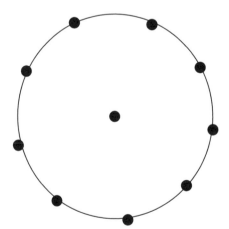

Nine-pin triangle

Learning through problem solving

Here the intention is to learn new mathematics *through* solving problems. The question that needs to be addressed is how can the range of needs of pupils in a group be met through this single starting point? What mathematics is it possible to cover?

It is possible to identify mathematical content from each of Years 7–11 and several examples are given below.

Year 7

The starting question might be:

How many different triangles are there in a 10-point circle (using the centre point and/or not using the centre point)? Describe how you know that the triangles are different. How many triangles are there in circles with different numbers of points (perhaps starting with an even number of points and asking pupils to generalise to an odd number of points later)?

Learning intentions: Begin to use line angle and symmetry properties of triangles and quadrilaterals; solve geometrical problems using these properties, using step-by-step deduction.

Year 8

The starting question might be:

What are the angles in the triangles formed in a 9-point circle, firstly with one vertex at the centre and then with each vertex on the circumference?

To solve this problem pupils will need to establish that the nine radii from the centre divide 360° into 9 equal angles of 40°. From this the angles of all isosceles triangles can be found and, in turn, the angles in any triangle with all its vertices on the circumference, by dissecting it into three isosceles triangles. This can be used as a starting point for a proof of some of the circle theorems met in the higher tier at Key Stage 4.

Learning intentions: Solve geometric problems using side and angle properties of equilateral, isosceles and right-angled triangles and special quadrilaterals, explaining reasoning with diagrams and text.

Year 9

Describe the properties of regular polygons that can be inscribed in different n-point circles. Which polygons can be drawn, and what are the sizes of their internal angles?

Consider families of triangles with one side equal in a particular point-circle. What do these triangles have in common and how might you prove the relationship?

Learning intentions: Solve problems using properties of angles, justifying inferences and explaining reasoning with diagrams and text. At the higher level in the Numeracy Framework it is suggested that pupils should distinguish between practical demonstration and proof.

Years 10 and 11

At this level, angle properties of circles can be discovered and then proved.

Learning intentions: Prove and use the facts that the angle subtended by an arc at the centre is twice the angle subtended by any point on the circumference.

What this demonstrates is the flexibility of this environment to be used at a very wide variety of levels and with a variety of outcomes. Although we have listed outcomes based on curriculum content expectations by year, from Years 7 to 11 it is perfectly possible that pupils will be working at all these levels in a mixed ability class. The environment also has the potential to be a far more stimulating and engaging way in which to learn circle theorems than the usual contexts offered (Andrews, 2002).

A completely open starter could be 'Investigate this environment, describe and justify what you discover' which leaves the pupils to extend their understandings and, with some mediation, extend their knowledge. Using the environment in the ways described above opens the possibility of learning mathematics *through* problem solving whilst extending the most able.

Learning about problem solving

The circular pegboard environment could also be used as a vehicle for learning *about* problem solving. By placing an emphasis on the stages of problem solving students can be helped to tackle the problems in a coherent and structured way. For example, they first need to understand what the problem is about and pull together the knowledge they already have that may be helpful. An approach to this is to encourage experimentation with the environment in order to get a picture of what might be happening. This would be followed by pupils working through examples they have identified in a very systematic way to check that an idea always appears to be true or to identify a pattern as a first stage to understanding why the pattern works; for example, finding the relationship between all the angles subtended by an arc at a point on the circumference might begin by drawing some triangles and finding angles by constructing isosceles triangles. From this the hypothesis, that the angles subtended at the circumference by the same length arc are always equal, might emerge. A systematic approach to trying different angles in different point circles may lead to a strong belief that this is always the case and also how to calculate in any circumstance what that angle might be. The final stage is then the proof; but the process of discovery has probably led to a structure for a proof or, at the least, a very convincing argument.

Such open environments also give pupils the opportunity to shine and latent talent to 'pop up out of the woodwork'. Discussion and evaluation of the different findings, the need to present convincing arguments to the group and a collaborative approach to learning will stimulate and encourage the brightest to 'find something new' and construct well-formulated arguments.

Example 2

The skill of being systematic and ordered when tackling a problem is not a trivial one but there are other underpinning mathematical thinking skills that support problem solving – such as generalising or the use of analogy – and all these skills need to be experienced and learned. Let us look at another example of a problem which contains some interesting mathematics that can be used with a mixed group and extend the most able whilst focusing on problem solving and the mathematical thinking skill of being systematic. Consider the following problem:

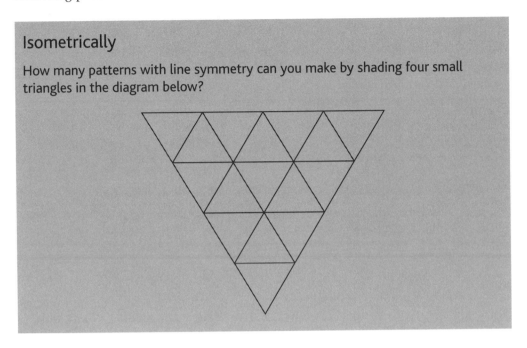

Isometrically

How many patterns with line symmetry can you make by shading four small triangles in the diagram below?

This problem requires a systematic consideration of all possibilities. A really organised approach will enable some generalisations and short cuts to be taken. There are a number of different approaches so there is ample room for discussion of methods that pupils try to use.

All the pupils can get started. Some, with little expertise in organising their thinking, will colour in randomly symmetric patterns to start with, some may need to revise their understanding of symmetry, and some will need to be nudged towards thinking about an organised approach to ensure that nothing has been left out. 'How will you convince me that you have all the patterns?' might be the question the teacher could ask to support pupils in thinking about how to tackle the problem in a systematic way.

In terms of problem solving strategies, pupils will therefore need to think about:

- what knowledge they already have that will be useful (knowledge of symmetry for instance)

- what constraints they will place on the problem (e.g. is it the same pattern if a rotation will give you an identical view?)

- would it be better to start with a simpler case (e.g. one triangle shaded and/or a smaller diagram)

- have they met anything like this before?

The problem solving process can be considered as the pupils progress discussing where they are and the sorts of things to try next. Discussion of the use of the skill of being systematic to convey a convincing argument of exhaustion is an important outcome. There is scope for the introduction of some new mathematics including combinatorics. For example, if no triangles along a line of symmetry are coloured how many other ways can the other four triangles be selected? The problem is extendable to any number of triangles (up to 16 of course).

Example 3

Take three from five

Choose any five numbers and find three whose sum is divisible by 3.

Can you guarantee that it is always possible to choose three numbers that will add up to a multiple of 3 from any group of five?

Can you explain why?

This appears to be true but why? Explanation can include discussion of divisibility rules, the partition of whole numbers into numbers of the form $3n$, $3n+1$ and $3n+2$ and permutations of three numbers from five. It is not essential to use algebra to produce a convincing argument but it is a natural development from the problem.

The problem could start with two from three – will it always be possible to find two numbers whose sum is even? It could be extended to 'four from ??' and so on. This problem has considerable scope at all levels and if introduced as a challenge from the teacher can be very motivating for pupils.

The focus on proof is a high-level skill but less able pupils can discuss what would be a convincing argument. In this respect, the problem can serve as a mechanism for developing algebraic proof and generalisability of a rule but it also requires the solver to be systematic in their examination of possibilities, so offers potential for working on problem solving skills. Finally, as a problem that can be used to reinforce and build on understandings of odds and evens, this is a lovely problem to tackle as a problem for its own sake. It is easy to step into so has a low threshold but has potential to extend the most able.

Example 4

Games with underpinning mathematical structure can provide very motivating starting points. Nim-like games offer scope for extension for more able pupils.

The game *Got it!* (which can be found on the the NRICH website – www.nrich.maths.org) involves an accessible strategy which can be generalised for any target number and any step numbers.

Got it!

This is an adding game for two. You play against the computer or against a friend.

Start with a target of 23. Set the range of available numbers from 1 to 4.

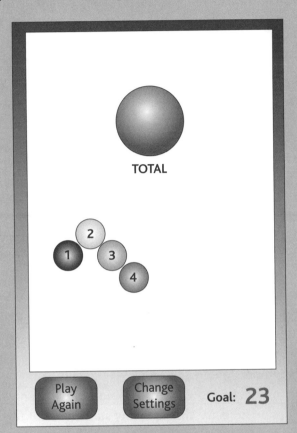

Players take turns to add a whole number from 1 to 4 to the running total.

The player who hits the target of 23 wins the game.

Play the game several times. Can you always win?

Can you find a winning strategy?

Does your strategy depend on whether or not you go first?

Change the game, choose a new *Got it!* target.

Test out the strategy you found earlier. Does it need adapting?

Can you work out a winning strategy for any target?

Is it best to start the game? Always?

Change the game again, returning to a target of 23 but using a different range of numbers this time.

Test out the strategies you found earlier. Do they need adapting?

Can you work out a winning strategy for any range of numbers? Is it best to start the game? Always?

Can you work out a winning strategy for any target and any range of numbers?

An extension to this game is *Last biscuit*:

Last biscuit

This is a game for two players. You will need 12 'biscuits', but perhaps something like buttons will be less fattening than real biscuits. Put four biscuits into one jar and eight into the other jar. (Just make the two groups.)

Each player can take biscuits in one of two ways:

1. by taking any number they like from just one jar or

2. by taking the same amount from both jars.

The winner is the person who takes the last biscuit.

This game has links to number sequences and involves some very interesting mathematics (more can be found on the NRICH website, www.nrich.maths. org.uk). The mathematics can be extended well beyond advanced level for those interested but identifying some of the winning positions and their relationships is a good start.

Games such as these can be stimulating and offer opportunities for conjectures and the production of convincing arguments (a stepping-stone on the way to formal proof). Pupils can be challenged to look at similar games and see what they can identify as connecting structures. There is scope for engagement at all levels from simply understanding the rules of the game and using some simple mental arithmetic to discovering winning positions, to guaranteeing a win from a particular starting point, to generalising to any starting point for a game.

Example 5: the traffic problem – a 'real world' context

The Department for Transport (DfT) have a document called 'A safer journey to school: a guide to school travel plans'. This guidance document for schools discusses ways in which they and their local authorities can work together to improve safety and is available through the site index on the home page (www.dft.gov.uk). The DfT have a number of resources that may be helpful but the aim of this project is to engage pupils in considering safety options to improve their journeys to school or the journeys of youngsters to the local primary school. Here are some of the points that are included as ideas for improving safety in the document:

*   At a raised junction the road is brought level with the pavement. Cars have to slow down while pedestrians can cross more comfortably.

*   Pinch points make the road narrower so the traffic slows down, while pedestrians don't have so far to cross.

*   Toucan crossings are like pelican crossings, but can be used by both pedestrians and cyclists.

- Cycle tracks can be routed away from the road or created along pavements or verges.

- Special motifs can be used to make a trail, guiding children along the safest routes.

- Road humps reduce speeds very effectively. They can have gaps at the side which allow cyclists to pass freely.

- Pedestrian refuges slow down traffic and allow pedestrians to cross the road in two stages. A dropped kerb makes it easier to cross.

- 20mph zones reduce pedestrian accidents and deter drivers from using the area as a rat-run.

- Chicanes are alternately spaced build-outs on opposite sides of the road that can slow vehicles down.

Pupils would be expected to examine existing provision and find out more about possible safety measures and assess the benefits and drawbacks to the school and the local community of their implementation. There is a large amount of information and data concerning journeys to school available on the internet which could also inform work on data handling. A project could focus on or use these facts and figures or those based on the school itself.

Amongst the questions pupils may seek to answer are:

- Where would you put parking restrictions or road bumps?

- Does traffic travel down the local roads at too high a speed?

- What is the volume of traffic? Could it be diverted along an alternative route?

- Are cycle tracks feasible and would they be used if built?

- What are the costs involved in building raised crossings or cycle tracks?

- Can the access to the school itself be improved to avoid congestion?

- Where will parents drop children if they come by car and how can you reduce the number of car journeys being made?

- What is the cycle track provision locally, can it be improved, how and at what cost? Is there any evidence to support any provision being used sufficiently to make the costs worthwhile?

- How can pupils' transport habits be amended to reduce the use of private cars?

- What is the volume of traffic outside the school at different times of the day and can this be related to school journeys?

- Where and how do students travel to school – what are the main routes and are they well serviced with crossings and traffic control measures?

Other subjects could be involved in such a project with pupils looking at safety in terms of stopping distances in wet and dry weather by devising an experiment to model cars stopping in various conditions and the effects of thinking times could involve the science department. A project focusing on getting messages across could be undertaken with art, English, media or PHSE departments.

This topic, like many others, has enormous potential to stretch and challenge the most able in an applied mathematical setting. In particular, the statistics aspect could be used to teach statistics content *through* the study rather than applying already learned knowledge.

Issues

> We haven't got time for problem solving – we've got to get through the syllabus.

Replacing normal lessons with problem solving lessons will not penalise pupils in standard tests. There is plenty of evidence to support this statement (Boaler, 1997; Watson *et al.*, 2003) and that it will result in high levels of motivation, engagement in the subject and greater likelihood that pupils will continue the subject post-16.

However, there are particular strategies for making time for problem solving by compacting the time spent on normal content instead of replacing it. This is achieved by looking vertically through the curriculum and identifying strands that can be taught in a single visit rather than through revisiting a theme several times over. A study using curriculum compaction at Key Stage 3 has been funded by the UK government (DfES and QCA, 2004). The models described in the guidance document include condensing the curriculum to support the less able as well as able pupils. It also contains models designed to make room for problem solving. Advantages are said to be:

- it empowers teachers to take control of what is taught and when

- the time created can be used to integrate problem solving back into the curriculum instead of either starting GCSEs early or simply running fortnightly problem solving sessions unrelated to the mathematics currently being studied.

It may also seem obvious that the circle activities above achieve exactly this: teaching properties of triangles and circles through problem solving. In fact, instead of taking more time, problem solving provides opportunities to combine strands into a single experience, in this case in a familiar – non-threatening – setting. Pupils can move from calculation using basic angle properties to most of the Euclidean circle geometry needed in the higher tier at GCSE.

Example 3 uses the partition of the whole numbers and modular arithmetic and proof that meets some of the requirements at advanced level. These are natural, unforced (though positively encouraged) developments which arise naturally out of good problems.

The teacher's role

Tackling the needs of the most able through problem solving approaches has implications for teaching as well as learning. The importance of the role of the teacher in any classroom where problem solving, problem posing and communication is at the core of learning cannot be overestimated. The delicate balance between letting things go and managing development is a difficult one that is handled in different ways by different teachers at different times. There is no single answer to this but problem solvers need to learn to be autonomous and independent. This does not mean isolated and uncommunicative. Mathematics is about communication and connections and this cannot happen in isolation; it requires pupils to feel part of a community of practice (Wenger *et al.*, 2002).

By modelling problem solving and sharing, and utilising pupils' ideas and approaches, the tools required for good problem solving can be taught by example and described explicitly. The description of process is very important in encouraging understanding of what is required. Problem solving is not a simple process but recent proposed changes to curriculum content and guidance materials is beginning to reflect this. An example of this complexity was offered by Schoenfeld (1985) who described four different ways of breaking a problem down:

- reducing the search space (number of possibilities)

- identifying useful mathematical facts or techniques that may help to solve part of the problem

- simplifying the task

- looking for patterns which can explain the underlying mathematics.

Unless some time is spent explaining the detail of what you mean when you say to students 'can we break the problem down' we should not be surprised when pupils struggle.

There are a number of examples of this complexity, and whilst we may not know in detail the nature of all possibilities, sharing what we might try next and the options available is a good first step. The example that springs to mind here is solving geometry problems, when we often expect pupils to scan (albeit often subconsciously) their bank of potentially useful facts (e.g. angles at a point, angles on a straight line, angle-sum of a triangle) to solve a problem.

In this environment, the teacher will not only be seen as the holder of knowledge of the subject but also as someone who has expertise in problem solving and who will share their knowledge and experiences with the pupils by problem solving *with* them. This is a departure from 'normal' views of the teacher. Clearly listening to, and valuing, opinions and pupils' attempts at creating convincing arguments is essential, not only for the teacher but for other pupils. In this way, they can begin to learn about mathematical precision. Other strategies that can support pupils in being mathematical include time for reflection (an explicit part of problem solving) which is also of value more generally in considering what individuals think they have come to understand, and where they think they may need to go next. Opportunities for metacognition, by pupils as well as teachers, can give focus to reflection and help the teacher in identifying misconceptions. The reflection might be oral or could take the form of learning diaries. Whilst we know that such reflection is good for all pupils, able pupils are particularly well placed to take advantage of such opportunities.

Kerry and Kerry (2000) talk of the classroom climate and they identify three prerequisites for a classroom where pupils are encouraged to learn:

- a climate of psychological security

- a climate that values intellectual activity

- a climate that encourages debate.

These prerequisites support pupils in feeling secure when they do not know as well as when they do, in sharing and testing ideas and being critical friends who talk about mathematics with confidence and realise that we can often learn as much from being wrong as being right. Again, whilst being good for all pupils, able pupils benefit particularly and comment on how they value such openness (Naisbett, 2003b).

Homework

Issues related to the purpose and value of homework are exactly the same for able pupils as any other pupil – to develop ideas and make connections. Homework is often set to consolidate, revise or prepare for new mathematics content or skills (including applications of mathematics) and for some pupils this will be by repeating similar tasks. For able pupils this is often tedious and unnecessary and they can be encouraged instead to use other sources for support and ideas, such as AskNRICH. They might already be taking part in masterclasses or lectures and workshops set up by other groups such as YG&T, ATM, RI and local HE institutions and one way of incorporating these back into a pupil's school experiences could be to invite them to report on, develop or share ideas met in these situations as a basis for homework.

Action research

Every day and in every lesson, we gain a sense of what seems to be working well and what is not. As teachers, we experiment and try to reflect critically on what happens in our lessons. One way of being more rigorous about your reflections and identifying what works for your pupils, and for you, is to critically examine what you try. To do this effectively you might consider undertaking some classroom-based action research through a professional development programme that will help you to frame your ideas clearly. Alternatively, pupils can be encouraged to keep reflective diaries where they describe their progress and feelings about the subject and their classroom experiences. Questionnaires, used once or twice a term, can give some targeted feedback. It is not necessary to undertake a rigorous analysis but these sources of information can shed some vital light on a student's changing views or concerns.

Resources

Resources are not simply about paper or the use of information and communications technology (ICT) or other equipment, but also about time and the people that are available to help. The role of teaching assistants can be very important in any model you adopt and they may well prove an excellent resource. In the same way, many universities now run outreach programmes which involve undergraduates and graduates coming into schools to support pupils and teachers. Such resources are invaluable, not only because of the opportunities they open up within the classroom but also as role models for pupils. It may also be the case that parents or friends of the school from local companies are willing to work with you in the classroom and, with the appropriate checks, they can bring views of the real world into the work being undertaken in the classroom.

Conclusion

The first question to ask is whether it is necessary or sufficient to treat able pupils differently and whether you will adopt an exclusive approach to teaching the most able. In this chapter, we have tried to develop a strong argument to say this is neither necessary nor sufficient. Able pupils need a community in which to work and share, and isolation does not support this. Even in a cohort of thirty or more able pupils, there is an enormous range of ability where different pupils will have different abilities in different topics or aspects of mathematics. The key question is will you give them different materials to work on, or the same?

This chapter has focused quite heavily on the role of problem solving and problem posing in supporting the needs of the most able through an inclusive approach to entitlement. We have also tried to give a sense of the complexity in what it means to be mathematical (which we believe is most closely reflected in settings where problems are at the core of the work). Problem solving is not something that can be taught on Friday afternoons or as part of coursework. It is an extensive aspect of mathematics and is worthy of significant attention, giving plenty of scope for able pupils to develop. In fact, serious consideration needs to be given for this complexity in depth and breadth to be realised in curriculum structures more generally. The recent report *Where Will the Next Generation of UK Mathematicians Come From* (Gardiner, 2005) emphasises the lack of such opportunities in the present curriculum. It is also easy to become distracted by curriculum and time pressures and consequently forget to share with our pupils such mathematical skills we have as teachers and which we tend to take somewhat for granted as we focus on facts and skills.

If you adopt an 'add on', exclusive approach to provision there is a large overhead in terms of resources for small numbers of pupils and, even with support, this is likely to be an unsustainable model.

There are many issues for administration and classroom practice and not least amongst the pressures on classroom practice are high stakes examinations. However, the evidence suggests that success in examinations and time spent on problem solving are not mutually exclusive and pupils can do as well if not better in standard tests when they spend time on problem solving. The bonus is their motivation and interest in the subject and the likelihood of them continuing to study mathematics post-16.

In the end there is little that you should be doing with your identified cohort that you should not be doing with everyone – what is good for able pupils is generally good education for everyone. In a sense, the identification has greatest value in helping you to monitor that you are meeting needs – in the same way as with low attaining pupils. Ultimately there needs to be sustained continuity and progression for each pupil, whether a solid and slow worker, or a real high flyer.

CHAPTER 5

Beyond the classroom

- Acceleration
- Enrichment and extension
- Competitions
- Other support for teachers

Introduction

Why do we need to be aware of opportunities to do mathematics outside the classroom, especially for our most able students? What do they have to offer? The first reason is obvious – there is a wealth of activities to supplement the classroom-based curriculum, many of which would be impossible or at least difficult to do in an ordinary classroom. The second is perhaps less practical and more philosophical – it is important for all pupils to be aware of mathematics in the outside world, but for those who are very able and possibly looking to use mathematics as a basis for a career, it's vital that we as mathematics teachers introduce and welcome our pupils into the community of mathematicians. Just as, for example, able musicians are introduced to playing with other able musicians in a variety of contexts and begin to build up a network of contacts and opportunities, so able mathematicians should have opportunities to experience doing mathematics within a wider community of practice.

The activities and resources below certainly do not constitute an exhaustive list. We have tried to give a flavour of what is out there, in the hope that it will inspire you to get 'googling' and find out what's available locally and nationally that would suit your pupils, and maybe you and your colleagues too. Where urls are given they are accurate as of June 2007.

Some are activities that are intended to be done in school in lesson time and sit well within the models of provision described in Chapter 4. However, these may still have a place beyond the classroom as either extension work or to complement classroom experiences.

Some could be done in school but might not fit so well into lesson time and may therefore be used as the focus for a club or other extracurricular activity. Such activities give pupils the chance to engage in a range of mathematical experiences, including working on novel contexts and meeting new mathematics, as well as giving pupils the chance to apply and consolidate existing knowledge.

Some activities take place well away from school, often at weekends or holiday times. Very able pupils who may be isolated in school often enjoy the opportunity to work with pupils of like ability or watch other people 'doing mathematics' or listen to others talking about mathematics. However, in these circumstances, it is often difficult to build follow-up activities back into the work of the classroom that utilise the experiences of those opportunities. This can mean that we do not make the most of the initial experience by developing it further, or sharing it with others. Time spent on preparing follow-up activities needs to be justified by making such activities part of a programme of regular events.

Some activities are closely linked to the National Curriculum and can be built on and connected to classroom work. Others stand alone and can be seen as topics which are of interest but may have limited connections to the curriculum and therefore may be perceived by the pupils as irrelevant and unrelated to their school experience. It is worth encouraging pupils in seeing the wider picture of mathematics so that they do not feel constrained by National Curriculum requirements. After all such experiences will make them more rounded, more capable mathematicians who see the power and pleasure mathematics has to offer.

We have chosen to order the resources according to the headings used in Chapter 4, but you will find many could have sat equally well elsewhere.

Acceleration

What is available?

Young Applicants in Schools Scheme (YASS)

YASS involves students studying a range of Open University courses equivalent to the first year of university level study and is recognised and supported by the DfES, the Specialist Schools Trust and, originally, NAGTY. The scheme is aimed at those who may have done particularly well in their GCSEs, who are highly motivated and who would benefit from being stretched academically. Modules currently being offered include, for example, 'Using Mathematics', 'Putting Computer Systems to Work' and 'Statistics in Society'. Credit can be transferred to their HE-level studies although they are not counted as points for entry to university.

The youngest pupils currently involved are 16–17-year-olds and they have to be selected through their school. There is a support system for pupils and teachers – some pupils undertake this work during regular school lessons alongside their teachers whilst others do it out of school time. There have been various studies of the scheme in practice and more information is available on the website – www.open.ac.uk/yass.

MEI 'Additional Mathematics'

In order to try to increase the number of able pupils taking AS/A level Mathematics in the sixth form, MEI are producing web resources to support the OCR 'Additional Mathematics' free-standing mathematics qualification. It is aimed at able Year 11 GCSE Mathematics students and is intended to be a bridge to AS Mathematics and beyond. It is equivalent in size to a single AS unit and carries UCAS points. The MEI web resources are written to work alongside the OCR 'Additional Mathematics' textbook and are intended to support students working independently, perhaps whilst the bulk of the class are concentrating on standard GCSE work. Additional Mathematics can be studied alongside GCSE Mathematics, or after an early-entry GCSE. For further details go to the MEI website – www.mei.org.uk.

In both the above cases, students report an increase in their self-confidence, an improvement in study skills and personal organisation. They have enjoyed encountering new subject areas and approaching familiar subject areas from a different standpoint.

Kumon

The Kumon scheme is a private after-school scheme in which pupils work through a series of graduated exercises. There is no overt reference to National Curriculum levels and pupils often work on different content to the work they are doing in school. The content includes, at the lowest level, practice of number algorithms, whilst at the highest level students can study negative numbers, algebra and equations, graphs, Pythagoras' Theorem, advanced algebraic skills, advanced functions, and differential and integral calculus. This means it is possible that, whilst some pupils will use the programme to support a mastery of basic skills, some may well study content in advance of their school peers, hence its inclusion here as an example of acceleration. For further information, visit the Kumon website – www.kumon.co.uk.

Examination support

There are several websites which support pupils taking higher mathematics examinations such as Further Mathematics A level and STEP papers.

Mathematics in Education and Industry (MEI), mentioned above, is an independent UK curriculum development body and runs the Further Mathematics Network, intended to make the Further Mathematics A level accessible to all students in schools and colleges in England. Some students take the examinations and use them as accreditation towards university entrance whilst others study the modules as helpful preparation but do not actually take the examinations. The network operates from regional centres through a mixture of intensive face-to-face teaching and self-study supported by online resources (see www.fmnetwork.org.uk). MEI also run the associated FM CPD course for teachers – see below under 'Support for teachers'. The MEI website also gives references for other useful online resources.

MES (Meikleriggs Educational Services) supports an open website which carries solutions to STEP (Sixth Term Examination Papers) papers and organises 'STEP forward' days for sixth-formers in the north-east as well as tuition for STEP and training for teachers – http://meikleriggs.org.uk.

The Cambridge University website also carries information about STEP questions – www.damtp.cam.ac.uk/user/stcs/STEP.html.

Enrichment and extension

What is available?

More maths grads

More maths grads is a £3.3 million programme designed to increase and widen participation within the mathematical sciences. It is funded by the Higher Education Funding Council for England (HEFCE) and is a collaboration between five mathematical organisations.

The three-year programme will see regional pilot schemes aiming to increase the number of students studying mathematics. It will also aim to encourage participation from groups of learners who have not traditionally been well represented in higher education, by helping school and college students understand why they are studying maths. A key aim of the project is to make maths enjoyable and this will help to improve students' confidence. This in turn will enable students to tackle problems that are more challenging and thus realise their potential in mathematics. Visit www.moremathsgrads.org.uk for more information.

Bletchley Park

Bletchley Park runs a website, competitions, visits and other events including some for teachers (www.bletchleypark.org.uk). Most activities and resources are concerned with codes and code breaking and a recent package entitled 'Codes & Ciphers' has been launched. The package is suitable for use by Key Stage 2/3/4 and A level teachers to help to incorporate and integrate topics on codes and ciphers from all spheres of life into their mainstream teaching.

Masterclasses

The Royal Institution (RI) supports secondary masterclasses which often take place at higher educational institutions on Saturday mornings. There are at present about 60 series of classes aimed at Year 8 or 9 students (12- to 14-year-olds). The RI also holds a series of free mathematics lectures for students at their London headquarters. Visit www.rigb.org for further information.

Other public lecture programmes are run by organisations including the Millennium Mathematics Project (www.mmp.maths.org).

Motivate

This is another project from MMP. One of the models adopted by the project involves several schools being video-linked to a mathematician who introduces a topic and leaves the pupils with problems based on the theme of their talk to work on over the subsequent weeks. At a later video-conferencing session, the students at the different schools exchange findings with each other and the mathematician, who gives them feedback. Visit www.motivate.maths.org for further information.

Regional partnerships

The National Academy for Gifted and Talented Youth (NAGTY) initially set up the Student Academy, offering summer schools and outreach activities, and a mathematics forum for its members on the website. The initial format was replicated in the nine regional partnerships (aligned to the government regional structure). The summer schools were a two weeks' residential activity. They were a mix of social events and mathematics which took place at various universities during the summer vacation. Topics were chosen to complement the school curriculum rather than accelerate pupils through it, and many of the pupils have continued to stay closely in touch with each other through the website. The extremely able pupils report enjoying talking mathematics with others of like interest and ability, something they seldom have the opportunity to do at school. Summer school provision will continue through the Excellence Hubs of the YG&T programme.

NRICH

Mentioned elsewhere, the NRICH website contains thousands of problems for pupils of all ages including sixth form students. The problems are a mixture of open and closed questions and are tagged so that they are easily linked to the National Curriculum – new ones are added each month. There are thousands of students worldwide who use the resource, some independently and others through school. Resources for teachers include articles about items of current interest and interactivities and games. Some teachers use the problems as classroom tasks whilst others use them as enrichment materials – the problem of the week for example, or as ideas for a mathematics club. For more information, visit www.nrich.maths.org.

Pupils might also enjoy using the 'AskNRICH' site where they can ask questions about any aspect of mathematics – the answers are provided (extremely promptly) by a team of students from Cambridge University (https://nrich.maths.org/discus).

SYMS

The Society of Young Mathematicians was started by the Mathematical Association in 1991 and organises maths events around the country. Young people under 18 can join and every term receive two maths magazines, *Symmetry Plus+* and *Mathematical Pie*, delivered direct to their homes. For further details, go to www.m-a.org.uk.

PLUS

Plus is an internet magazine which aims to introduce the beauty and the practical applications of mathematics. There are feature articles which describe applications of mathematics to real-world problems, games and puzzles; reviews of popular mathematics books and events; a news section, showing how recent news stories are often based on some underlying piece of mathematics; and opinions on various mathematics-related topics and news stories. A regular feature is the interview with someone in a mathematics-related career, showing the wide range of uses mathematics is put to in the real world. All past issues remain available online. For further information, go to http://plus.maths.org.

Roadshows

Both the Millennium Mathematics Project (MMP) and the Liverpool Mathematical Society take roadshows into schools. Whilst they are aimed at the full ability range, many teachers find that they often act as a stimulus for the most able who continue working at the problems and puzzles. More information is available from http://mmp.maths.org/projects/roadshow.html and www.maths.liv.ac.uk/lms.html.

Villiers Park

Villiers Park, an educational charity, runs extension courses for pupils – the latest is entitled 'Mathematics: Chaos or Clear-Cut?' Also on offer are residential week-long courses for sixth form students who are intending to study mathematics at university, probably aiming for Oxbridge entrance. The courses are very popular and competition for places is strong. For further information, go to www.villierspark.org.uk.

World Class Arena

The World Class Tests were originally devised by QCA and they can now be taken online. The problems are intended to be difficult in that they require the student to make connections across different areas of mathematics (and also for the problem solving tests, science and design and technology) but do not expect any knowledge in advance of that expected for the chronological age of the child. Teaching and learning materials (Mathinsight and problem solving modules) have been developed – most of them are low threshold, high ceiling tasks which can be used as whole-class activities but have potential for greater challenge for the most able. The tests can be found at www.worldclassarena.org.

Competitions

What is on offer?

The mathematics challenges

The United Kingdom Mathematics Trust (UKMT) organises challenges which are tests of reasoning and mental agility which can be taken without any special preparation or revision. The three levels cover the secondary school range 11–18 and together they attract over half a million entries each year from over 4000 schools and colleges.

The junior and intermediate challenges are aimed at the top 35% of pupils in each year group. The senior challenge is suitable for all students aged 16–19 studying mathematics below university level. Enthusiastic younger pupils are also encouraged to enter the challenges. The Team Mathematics Challenge is a national mathematics competition for teams of four pupils in Years 8 and 9 (or equivalent). It is designed to promote team working and provide a stimulating challenge to students working in groups. The challenges are practical tasks as well as theoretical problems. Further information on both sets of challenges can be found on the UKMT site at www.ukmt.org.uk.

The Scottish Maths Challenge also offers very challenging questions and you can find out more and see sample competition questions at www.maths.mcs.st-andrews.ac.uk/~smc.

The Mathematics Olympiad

Each November, invitations to the British Mathematical Olympiad are sent to pupils who score highly in the Senior UKMT Challenge, although it is sometimes possible for teachers to enter other pupils who they think would benefit from the experience. The qualifying score appears on the website as soon as possible after the Senior Challenge to help teachers in assessing which pupils to enter. The paper for Round One lasts three and a half hours and contains six complex and involved mathematical problems for which full written solutions are required. High achievers in Round One (usually held in early December) are invited to try Round Two (usually held in early February). The BMO plays an important role in identifying the UK team for the annual International Mathematical Olympiad (http://imo.math.ca).

Other local competitions

Enterprising Mathematics Competition is a Scottish competition in which heats are held throughout the country and the winning teams of 14–15-year olds take part in the National Final. Information is available at www.maths.mcs.st-andrews.ac.uk/~smc.

Edge Hill College's annual challenge involves about 250 teams of Year 9 pupils. Contact the maths subject administrator at Edgehill on 01695 584329 or email fellerst@edgehill.ac.uk.

Southampton University runs an annual cipher challenge – www.cipher.maths.soton.ac.uk.

Other support for teachers

National Centre for Excellence in the Teaching of Mathematics

Set up in 2006, the NCETM offers a national infrastructure for subject-specific professional development for teachers of mathematics. Its aim is to strengthen the teaching and learning of mathematics. Built around a web portal (www.ncetm.org.uk), it offers information on conferences and professional development courses nationally, discussion forums and communities, as well as resources to support pedagogical development. In addition to the portal there is a network of regional coordinators covering all of England. Each regional coordinator is working to create local networks, build relationships with mathematics teachers and organisations, identify opportunities for high quality professional development and share examples of excellence across their region.

Conferences

ATM and MA

These are probably the most well known conferences for teachers, held annually during the Easter vacation. They are opportunities to meet other teachers, student teachers and researchers and do some mathematics too. Further information can be found at www.m-a.org.uk and www.atm.org.uk.

British Society for Research into Learning Mathematics (BSRLM)

BSRLM runs Saturday conferences and produces reports of the proceedings – www.bsrlm.org.uk.

The Institute of Mathematics and its Applications (IMA)

IMA organises conferences introducing teachers to some of the areas where mathematics is used in the world of work – www.ima.org.uk/institute/aboutus.htm.

The Institute of Physics and the Royal Society

These institutions have begun holding joint conferences and seminars, bringing together teachers of physics and mathematics in secondary schools and colleges. The aim is to identify strategies that could improve the links between the two subjects in schools to their mutual benefit. For further information, go to www.iop.org.

Bridges: Mathematical Connections in Art, Music, and Science

Bridges conferences have been held annually since 1998. Their aim is to bring together artists (of all types) and mathematicians for talks and discussions to identify and provide opportunities to present their work, meet each other and exchange ideas. They also offer encouragement and inspiration to teachers of mathematics at all levels by revealing relationships between mathematical subjects and their artistic/aesthetic presentations. For more information, visit www.lkl.ac.uk/bridges.

Courses

Villiers Park

Villiers Park is an educational charity which runs CPD courses for teachers. Recent mathematics courses have included Enriching AS/A2 Level Teaching. For more information, visit www.villierspark.org.uk.

ATM

ATM organise activity-based courses to enrich mathematics teaching at Key Stages 2, 3 and 4. For more information, go to www.atm.org.uk/courses/index.html.

MA

The MA has local branches and runs activities and CPD courses about teaching able pupils – www.m-a.org.uk.

Teaching Advanced Mathematics (TAM)

This is a seventeen-month course, incorporating two summer holidays, designed to give teachers the skills and confidence to teach A level Mathematics. It is run by the MEI project (www.mei.org.uk).

NRICH

The NRICH team run a range of flexible courses in local centres – go to http://nrich.maths.org and follow the link to courses.

General websites

G&TWise

This website is a searchable database of resources covering all curriculum areas including mathematics. The database includes paper-based resources, competitions, roadshows, websites, curriculum materials, etc. and is intended to be a 'one-stop-shop' for gifted and talented support. The database is growing all the time and input from users with good ideas is welcomed. Visit www2.teachernet.gov.uk.

CHAPTER 6

Case studies

- Compacting the Key Stage 3 curriculum
- Primary–secondary transition
- Continuing professional development
- Cross-curriculum and support for other subjects
- Provision beyond the school
- Home–school liaison
- Underachieving mathematicians
- Bullying
- Dual exceptionality
- Asperger syndrome
- Exceptionally able

In this chapter we consider what might actually happen in schools. The case studies are all based on our experiences of working and talking with colleagues and pupils in secondary schools, and so each is a composite picture drawn to illustrate best practice. Each case study is followed by a selection of potentially useful contacts and/or resources.

Case study 1 – compacting the Key Stage 3 curriculum

Context

School G is a large, oversubscribed 11–18 comprehensive school, drawing pupils from a wide geographic area covering a broad social and ethnic mix. Maths GCSE and A level results have been above the national average for a number of years. In mathematics, pupils are split into two half-year bands. In Year 7 there are 4 sets in each band, each set having between 25 and 32 pupils. In each half of the year, the department has previously managed with three sets, but the growing intake has precipitated the change, and the smaller set size has been a factor in the department being prepared to think more imaginatively about provision. The department has seven full-time staff and a number of part-time staff. All but four of the teaching staff have a mathematics related degree. In previous years, the department, mainly driven by a school-wide policy, has targeted pupils likely to fail at GCSE and those on the C–D borderline with some success. Although results improved significantly as a result of these interventions, there is some concern that, more recently, improvements have slowed considerably.

The situation

Able pupils appear to be coasting and losing motivation in Years 8 and 9. The uptake of mathematics post-16 is declining with Further Maths under threat because of falling numbers, despite the fact that the school roll is growing. GCSE results do not appear to be improving as much as the department would like.

The story

The problem was identified by the head of department, H, at a departmental meeting at the start of an academic year. E, an established member of the department, had been on a course the previous term on using problem solving. E described to the department the enthusiasm she felt just 'doing some mathematics' and talked about doing mathematics with other colleagues on the course. She felt that, by introducing some problem solving into the curriculum, pupils might be more motivated and start to talk about maths 'just like they talk about a book in English'. There was a lot of discussion, including concerns about the time needed to implement problem solving. J mentioned the discussions that had taken place on his PGCE course concerning curriculum compaction and suggested that looking at what was being taught with a view to 'efficiency' might release some time for problem solving or something similar. H asked the department to give this some thought and possibly do some research and agreed that the department would discuss this a little more in the next meeting.

Between meetings H arranged to see his link on the senior management team (SMT) to discuss what the school's policy might be on curriculum compaction, early entry to GCSE (although H was not convinced this was where he wanted to go) and how his department might be supported if they wanted to pilot an innovation. Some weeks later, the member of the SMT indicated that there was some interest in what might be possible and if H could work out and present something to a management team meeting, including suggested resource implications, they could make an informed decision.

At the next department meeting, the main item was 'supporting the most able'. With the help of E and J, H collected a range of information together including guidance on *A Condensed Key Stage 3* (DfES and QCA, 2004) and some literature on problem solving. This was circulated before the meeting. H also invited the link member of the SMT to join them.

The outcome of the meeting was a decision to implement a condensed Key Stage 3 by reviewing the curriculum content but with a view to integrating problem solving across the three years in the time that was created. There would be no early entry. It was agreed that they would start in Year 7 and not try to implement anything new with older pupils who were established into a certain way of working. This would mean that they did not have to do everything at once. To start with, they would pick one or two topics a term to base around problem solving and would target one group.

The department also agreed, in consultation with the member of SMT, that as the intake was due to grow again next year, they should ask the SMT to support an additional set in each band to relieve the pressure and ensure that a more targeted group of pupils could be identified. If this was agreed, the project would go ahead. A member of the department responsible for liaison with primary schools would ask feeder schools to 'recommend' pupils to be included in the pilot, based on some input from the department on the nature and content of the course later in the year.

The consultation process with the SMT was successful and in the spring term work began on designing the scheme of work for the following year. The work was led by E and J, and included two staff development days which focused on problem solving and the new scheme of work. The aim was that everyone should be aware of what was happening and could contribute. Work would be ongoing in the next year but, very early on, they realised that in order to compact or condense the curriculum they would have to look at all three years (and beyond) so they were effectively planning content for all three Key Stage 3 years a topic at a time. Content was initially covered in the same order as previously so movement between sets was still possible. The curriculum was compacted first and then particular topics were chosen as the problem solving focus. These included:

- number – factors and multiples and triangular and square numbers

- use of symbolic notation to support generalising and the idea of simplification

- coordinates

- area.

In fact, some adjustment was necessary as the chosen problem solving contexts sometimes covered more than one area of the curriculum. This had a knock-on effect for the ordering of topics across the whole of Year 7, for example coordinates and area were put adjacent to each other.

Commentary including outcomes and next steps

The ability to be far more flexible in the delivery of the Key Stage 3 framework has generally become rather lost in its implementation. However, this flexibility is open to everyone, whether one adopts a compaction model which frees time for early entry to GCSE or, as with some schools, with the aim of starting Key Stage 3 content later to give less able pupils a chance to become more confident with Key Stage 2 content.

The main benefit of any reflective practice is the opportunity to take ownership of what you are teaching your pupils and feel more 'at home' with the story you are trying to share. In reviewing the Key Stage 3 content, for whatever purpose, teachers come to know the landscape and are not focused so much on the tree in the foreground that they do not notice how it fits into its surroundings.

Some particular comments about, and outcomes of, the case study:

- It is difficult to move pupils across sets because of the different styles being adopted.

- There are implications for teaching approaches and staff development time is needed.

- Teachers involved in problem solving approaches are beginning to use problem solving elsewhere in their teaching.

- Evidence suggests improved pupil attitudes and motivation.

There is a need to consider whether the approach should not be restricted to the most able groups because:

- there is a considerable amount of flexibility in outcome in the problem solving settings

- the very able can fly whilst others are working on more elementary maths

- everyone can discuss the mathematics, conjecture and try to justify what they are finding

- there are implications for assessment for learning and monitoring.

Looking forward there needs to be:

- a means of collecting evidence concerning attitudes, engagement and motivation

- a mechanism for obtaining feedback from parents

- a consideration of the implications for GCSE course planning.

There is also considerable potential here for some action research.

Guidance

A Condensed Key Stage 3: Designing a Flexible Curriculum (DfES Ref: 0798-2004) is also available to download from www.standards.dfes.gov.uk.

Case study 2 – primary–secondary transition

Context

School K is a large, oversubscribed inner-city 11–18 comprehensive school, drawing pupils from a large number of primary schools. In each year there are eight maths classes, set after the January of Year 7. There is a high level of parental involvement and support.

The situation

At a recent Year 7 parents' evening several staff were asked about the policy of having mixed ability classes in Year 7 as some children were said to be disappointed and bored for much of the first term because they were repeating work they had done in Year 6. The maths department decided it was time to look more closely at the partnership they had with their primary schools, which had always been hit and miss because of the number and variety of partner schools they had to work with.

The story

The school had previously tried using the QCA maths bridging units with the partner primary schools but with limited success. Some of the schools were very committed to working in partnership and had undertaken the units with great enthusiasm whilst others were unconvinced of their value. Because of the difficulty of communicating with so many primary schools and receiving incomplete information about the new pupils, the maths department had decided to set up mixed ability classes in Year 7 until they had got to know the pupils well enough to set them by ability. The comments at parents' evening were received without much surprise as most of the staff felt that the first term was spent revising topics from Year 6 in order to reassess the pupils and gain some idea of their ability in order to put them into ability sets. At the departmental meeting they decided to try to think of some alternative ways of giving all the new pupils a positive experience over the transitional period, but with the proviso that whatever new ideas they came up with had to be realistic, manageable and informative.

The G&T coordinator indicated that there would be a small sum of money available for liaison with primary schools. The maths colleague with responsibility for Year 7, G, was happy to lead this initiative and researched the literature on effective transition. She concluded that one of the key factors missing in the relationship that this particular school had with partnership schools was a lack of trust in professional judgements. This had led to the maths department retesting all the pupils in Year 7 in order to confirm what information they had received from the primary school, where such information existed.

As a pilot project she and two other members of staff who taught Year 7:

(a) contacted all of the feeder schools and asked to be invited into Year 6 maths classes to observe

(b) set up an after-school partnership for all the Year 6 teachers, Year 7 teachers and G&T coordinators to discuss the current situation and make suggestions for future plans.

This was the beginning of a professional dialogue in which all schools except two (primaries) were involved. The teachers planned a rota of exchange visits and termly meetings during which topics of mathematical interest would be discussed from the point of view of continuity and progression across key stages.

Commentary including outcomes and next steps

Transition between primary and secondary schools has been criticised frequently over the last few years. Within the Excellence in Cities initiative, improving transition for able pupils across the Key Stage 2/3 divide is a specific target and secondary schools are supposed to work towards partnership with their feeder primary schools both in exchange of information and in organising activities across the Year 6/7 groups. In a recent Ofsted report, secondary schools in general were described as

> not building well enough on what their Year 7 pupils had achieved in English and mathematics in Year 6. They generally did not know, in sufficient detail, what their new pupils could do, and they had not set targets for improving attainment during Year 7. Partner primary and secondary schools generally had little knowledge of their respective practices in assessing and recording progress and in setting targets. The National Literacy and Numeracy Strategies have improved the monitoring of pupils' progress towards targets set at Key Stage 2. Little of this valuable information was finding its way to secondary school English and mathematics departments, however, and too much time was spent by secondary schools filling gaps by testing pupils at the beginning of Year 7. There was insufficient discussion between teachers in Key Stages 2 and 3 about the standards of work expected of pupils and about approaches to teaching. The standards which are ignored most are those achieved by higher attaining pupils.
> (Ofsted, 2003a)

The six key factors in effective transition were identified in the same report as:

- effective transfer of information

- effective dissemination of information

- use of information

- professional trust – accuracy of assessments

- non-duplication of work/testing, etc.

- shared expectations/targets.

School K had identified one of these, professional trust, as being crucial in establishing good relationships between staff. From other research (National Primary Trust, 1999) we know that the other factors are important too, but a personal relationship between teachers, in which a dialogue about mathematics is shared, is one of the most effective ways of ensuring continuity of curriculum and experience for their pupils.

Schools do establish strong relationships in different ways. Some schools find the time and resources to exchange teachers from primary to secondary as well as vice versa, especially in the last term of the year when assessments are over and the secondary timetable is possibly less full. The secondary teachers benefit by getting to know the abilities of the Year 6 pupils whilst the Year 6 teachers understand the progression into Key Stage 3. And of course, the Year 6 pupils get to know one of their new maths teachers. However, some Year 6 teachers are not happy teaching Year 7 (especially able Year 7) and prefer to observe or team-teach rather than take responsibility for the lessons. Such activity also supports shared expectations and shared target setting, which is another of the key factors.

Some schools use a common piece of work as a thread to connect Year 6 and Year 7, sometimes even using the same workbook, starting it at the end of Year 6 and continuing with it at the beginning of Year 7. This was the idea behind the transition or bridging units which had been unsuccessful in school K, dependent as they are on all the primary schools joining in, or the choice of topic being such that pupils can easily catch up if they have come from schools which have not undertaken the work. An innovative version of this was used by schools in the Bedfordshire area who devised online units that could be monitored by primary and secondary teachers alike. You can read more about this on the DfES website (www.dfes.gov.uk).

In both of these cases the teachers' understanding of pupils of all abilities is likely to increase, but here we are trying to focus on the most able because we know that they are the ones worst served by transition. Special needs pupils are likely to be well served because the communication with and between special educational needs coordinators (SENCOs) is generally effective. The middle ability pupils will be well served because it will be assumed correctly that they have achieved an average attainment – level 4. But the most able are potentially the most vulnerable as their abilities are likely to be underestimated.

The other key factors for effective transition centre on information:

- *what* is transferred – just national test results, or a more in-depth description of a pupil's abilities, or a portfolio of exceptional work, etc. What additional information about very able pupils might be useful? What is manageable to produce and interpret?

- *how* it is transferred – electronically, on paper, in an accepted format (such as the Common Transfer Document available on the DfES website). Does such a format provide for information about high ability to be communicated?

- how is the information *disseminated* and to whom – in primary schools one class teacher can hold all of the information about a pupil. In secondary schools the information might go to the head of Year 7, the head of maths, the G&T coordinator, the Year 7 tutors, etc. If there is no effective strategy for passing on information, then the maths department needs to be proactive in seeking it out.

- *what happens* to the information once it has been passed on – there are stories of filing cabinets with information that has never been looked at. Information is only useful if it informs future actions. This may be to set pupils immediately on arrival in secondary school (although the effectiveness of that is open to a different discussion). It may be to alert staff that in their mixed ability class they have some very able pupils, and to ensure that they are provided with a challenging curriculum from the start.

There are other examples of good practice which are incidental to mathematics but nevertheless worth bearing in mind. This list comes from another Ofsted document, based on examples of good practice seen in schools around the country.

- Consider methods of helping children to understand the differences between teaching methods at Key Stage 2 and Key Stage 3.

- The sending of newsletters from the secondary school to inform Year 6 pupils and their teachers of the events and activities organised in Key Stage 3.

- A 'moving on' booklet, initiated by the LA (local authority), in which pupils write about themselves and complete activities related to changing schools.

- Correspondence between Year 6 and Year 7 pupils to enable new entrants to ask questions about experience in Year 7.

- Follow-up receptions for Year 6 teachers to meet Year 7 pupils to discuss the experience of changing schools.

- Mentoring and 'buddy' systems can help with both the pastoral and academic aspects of transition.

- Joint secondary and primary school events have worked well in some areas.

- Questionnaires for both primary and secondary pupils can help to gather an overall picture of what works and what doesn't work in supporting pupils through the transition period (Ofsted, 2002).

Guidance

Transition units for English and Maths can be found on the DfES's Standards site. Scroll down to Targeted Support and click on Transition Units (www.standards.dfes.gov.uk/primary/publications/mathematics/12838/ks3_trans_y6toy7maths03ed_a.pdf).

Information on the Common Transfer File can be found in TeacherNet's Management area – www.teachernet.gov.uk.

E2BN network materials on setting up online transition projects can be found at http://web.e2bn.net/db/manual_pdf/01_trans.pdf.

The following organisations can also provide guidance on transition

- the Association for Achievement and Improvement through Assessment: Crossing the Bridge case studies – www.aaia.org.uk

- University of Cambridge Faculty of Education Transfer and Transition Project – http://creict.homerton.cam.ac.uk/transfer

- Suffolk Education Transition in Education – www.slamnet.org.uk/ transfer/#edp.

Case study 3 – continuing professional development

Context

School J is a large, oversubscribed 11–16 comprehensive school, drawing pupils from a wide geographic area covering a broad social and ethnic mix. Maths GCSE results have been below national average for a number of years despite numerous strategies to provide additional support to pupils. It has been difficult to recruit maths staff and the department has several teachers for whom mathematics is a second or even third curriculum area that they teach.

The situation

The non-specialist maths teachers are, unsurprisingly, less confident and less competent than their specialist peers are. Historically they have been allotted low ability sets, in which behaviour is often a problem too, rather than higher ability sets where their own maths ability may be called into question. The recently appointed head of department, P, would like to raise the confidence and competence of the department so that all can take a share in teaching low and high ability groupings.

The story

Since P arrived he has been thinking about ways of improving the confidence and knowledge base of his department, and is also keen to put in place some support mechanisms for those colleagues who need it. The department functions well socially but there is no history of maths CPD (continuing professional development) other than the recent Key Stage 3 strategy days and the occasional feedback on examination entries. P feels there needs to be a longer-term embedded strategy to improve the teaching skills of colleagues. He uses the department's CPD money to take the whole department to a local Saturday conference at which the focus is on 'teachers doing maths'. This was very successful and most of the teachers came back enthused. For some it was the first time they had done any maths themselves for a very long time, in some cases since they were at school! Building on this, P planned to use half of each term's INSET day to do some maths, followed by a session entitled 'planning for challenge'.

Commentary including outcomes and next steps

The non-specialist teachers in P's school were not unusual in rarely having done any maths of their own, for pleasure. This seems to be a particular characteristic of many maths departments and unlike other departments in the school. For example, many sports teachers are themselves involved in playing or coaching sport outside school, music teachers frequently go to concerts, or play in amateur orchestras, or spend time listening to music for pleasure. Art teachers often are practising artists themselves, and it would be difficult to find an English teacher who didn't enjoy reading for pleasure! But in maths departments, it is, unfortunately, unusual to find colleagues who are enthused by maths for its own sake.

It is important that able pupils in particular have exposure to those with high levels of expertise and this is recognised as one of the key issues in gifted and talented education (Sternberg in Meunier, 2003). Of course for all pupils it is important to be taught by those who are knowledgeable about their subject, but for the most able we are talking of specific ways of further developing their own expertise – of helping them to think like a mathematician. The CPD initiative offered by P allowed his colleagues to experience what it was like to work like a mathematician, and P's hope was that they would then be able to model this sort of behaviour when they were teaching.

The story continued

All his colleagues enjoyed the INSET day and, once they had overcome their initial insecurity, even the least confident contributed to the discussions about classroom practice. Although they did not feel confident enough to offer to work with the more able groups, they were happy to go along with the idea of continuing to have some maths as an ongoing interest in the faculty room. The biggest surprise to P was the reaction of the established teachers, who became reinvigorated and took responsibility for setting a problem of the week which was aimed at the pupils, but which became a topic of conversation for the staff too. Over the course of the next year's INSET sessions different teachers took turns to present interesting investigations or problems and this was followed by discussions about how, when and why such activities might be used in the classroom. Although there was no noticeable improvement in results immediately, P is convinced that this immersion in maths will have longer-term effects on the teaching and hence on the learning.

Guidance

INSET sessions are organised through, amongst others:

- Association of Teachers of Maths – www.atm.org.uk

- Mathematical Association – www.m-a.org.uk

- Stands for Education (SfE) – www.sfe.co.uk

- National Academy for Gifted and Talented Youth – www.nagty.ac.uk

- Villiers Park Educational Trust – www.villierspark.org.uk

- United Kingdom Mathematics Trust (UKMT) – www.ukmt.org.uk

- NRICH – www.nrich.maths.org.uk.

Case study 4 – cross-curriculum and support for other subjects

Context

School D is a small, four-form entry, 11–18 comprehensive in an urban area. It has a small sixth form with many subjects taught across a consortium with three other local comprehensives. There is a new head of mathematics who is keen to look at cross-curriculum activities between mathematics, science and geography. He has built up some strong links with these departments in terms of making connections with work pupils are doing in other subjects when teaching topics in the mathematics lessons.

The need/problem

R, a Year 11 very able mathematician and scientist, needs some additional help with her science that could be met with the help of the mathematics department.

The story

R is working well ahead of her peers in science and mathematics.

In science R has chosen to do some mechanics as an additional topic as she is interested in engineering and so this topic has particular appeal to her. She is working through some A level material and has some one-to-one time with one of the science staff after school every week. In lessons, she either works with the group on a topic or works on her own. The decision on what to do is a joint one made with the teacher in advance in the regular Wednesday meeting they have.

In mathematics, R often joins in with the normal work of the lesson but often finishes early and the teacher always has something 'up his sleeve'. Most of the additional work R has been doing in maths relates to proof and problem solving.

R is encouraged to attempt some formal proofs related to the general work of the group. She has met most of the techniques taught at A level, including proof by induction, which she finds particularly 'weird' and slightly discomforting. Techniques are taught when needed in lessons, or informally either in lunch sessions or after school on a semi-regular basis. The nice thing about the choice of proof as an enrichment topic was that it could support almost all the topics she was doing and it was teaching her what it was like 'to be mathematical', which fits in with R's longer term ambitions. R's maths teacher was beginning to think about what might be a good next step.

At break in the staff room, R's maths and science teachers were discussing R. She was in the first term of Year 11 and was keener than ever. The science teacher mentioned that things were getting rather difficult because R really needed to do some calculus and he was finding it difficult to see how he could fit this into the Wednesday slot and he was not terribly confident that he would do a good job. The obvious solution to both teachers was that this could form the next focus for R's mathematics enrichment. In fact, the Year 12 mathematicians were just about to start this as a topic and the mathematics teacher wondered whether it might be possible for R to join the group for the first couple of weeks to get her started and then she could do some independent study with the usual support. There were some excellent resources around too that could help.

A meeting was arranged with R's form tutor, the G&T coordinator and the Year 11 manager. It was agreed that, provided staff teaching the subjects that would be affected by R joining the A level group were in agreement, and if this was what R wanted to do, they could go ahead with the plan for R to join the group for between two and three weeks.

The staff affected agreed to release R (with the usual proviso concerning catching up with missed work). The arrangement worked very well and the collaboration over mathematics and science became well established with regular meetings across coffee to discuss what was coming up next and how they could support each other and R, who gained greatly by the collaboration.

Commentary including outcomes and next steps

This small-scale collaboration worked because:

- the teachers involved were able to communicate

- R's needs had been identified and efforts were being made to support those needs

- the departments were able to get funding for additional materials to support R

- the use of themes for extension made the system manageable, although the reliance to some extent on the 'good will' of the teachers involved is not entirely satisfactory and this needs addressing, with some recognition or additional support for the work involved. The use of a mentor from outside the school may have been one way of helping.

R enjoyed the autonomy and working independently and had the skills to do this – other pupils might need a lot more support.

Guidance

The following sites contain useful resources:

- Mathsnet – www.mathsnet.net

- MathCentre – www.mathcentre.ac.uk.

MEI has links to a number of other resources – www.mei.org.uk.

Case study 5 – provision beyond the school

Context

School E is an 11–18 comprehensive school where AS and A2 mathematics are very popular. Several other local schools do not have such vibrant numbers doing advanced level and attempts have been made in the past, with varying degrees of success, to run a consortium arrangement, particularly for A2. Within the consortium, most of the teaching is done by staff in school E because of their previous experiences. The A level maths groups are based loosely on GCSE results and recommendation from previous schools.

The need/problem

In this large and oversubscribed school, mathematics is a popular subject and results at AS and A2 are good. Students regularly take mathematics related subjects at university but as a percentage of those studying the subject the number is low. The school takes students from a wide catchment area with a consequent variety in their experiences up to A level. The school needs to develop a range of strategies for linking with Higher Education.

The story

Students who are successful in their application to join the sixth form to do mathematics at advanced level receive a welcome pack in the summer break with some suggested pre-course materials to work on. The aim is mainly to have a common experience for all the students when they arrive so they have something to discuss and share fairly early in the course. The pack also contains information on the sorts of courses students have undertaken after they finish at the school, so right from the start students are aware of a wide range of possible options.

The mathematics department is currently involved in or positively encourages a range of links including:

- university undergraduates coming to the school each week during term time to work with the students, supporting the teachers and acting as role models, as well as being someone to talk to about doing mathematics or a related topic at university

- the department has one or two talks each year from lecturers, normally from the local university but sometimes from further afield and some specifically linked to maths related careers

- ex-students also return to talk about their courses

- students are told of public lectures run at the local university by the Royal Institution

- there have been a number of video-conferences involving a talk and tasks set by a mathematician

- the school encourages students to attend university-based summer schools in the summer following their first year

- the department encourages the use of discussion forums (such as AskNRICH – mentored by university undergraduates) which can support students when they are struggling with particular concepts or who are looking beyond the course content or who simply want to find out more about mathematics at university or STEP (Sixth Term Entrance Papers).

The school has also managed to identify a link mentor at the local university. So far, the mentor has been in to talk to some students interested in taking maths related degrees but she has also made regular visits, about once a month, to work with a group of very able students doing some of the first year degree course topics.

The school is currently considering:

- the use of YASS courses for very able students. In the past very able students have tended to undertake additional units at advanced level. Staff feel that this tends to be more of the same. Additional units are also difficult to support and YASS can be done in the students' own time. A major advantage is the development of independent study skills.

- some integration into the MEI Further Mathematics project as a means of supporting students who have not chosen to do a full mathematics A level but wish to do a couple of modules to support their other subjects.

Commentary including outcomes and next steps

The school is developing links that both inform and support students. There is an outward looking ethos where students are encouraged to look ahead and enquiries concerning the need for advice on courses, or things students can do to support their work and areas they are interested in, are followed up with advice or action or a contact that can help. By making links with outside agencies a natural part of the student's experiences the expectation to look beyond the school is implicit and an accepted part of the preparation for the subject post-18.

Guidance

Students are entered for STEP by the OCR examination board – www.ocr.org.uk. Further guidance is available from www.cam.ac.uk/admissions/undergraduate/tests/step.html. Example solutions can be found at http://meikleriggs.org.uk.

Advice from students who have taken STEP papers can be found at http://nrich.maths.org/askedNRICH/edited/menu/step.html.

Additional guidance is available from the following organisations:

- YASS – www3.open.ac.uk/courses/search/yass.shtm

- TAM – www.mei.org.uk/tam.shtml

- MEI – www.mei.org.uk.

Case study 6 – home–school liaison

Context

School B is an 11–16 comprehensive school situated in a semi-urban area. It is a relatively small school with a full ability range, although proportionally it has fewer very able pupils than one might expect due to the mix of selective and comprehensive schools in the area. The needs of pupils identified as gifted and talented are overseen by the school's G&T coordinator who is not a member of the mathematics department. The school has a policy on home–school liaison and the mathematics department is expected to be fully aware of the policy and its implementation. One of the key features of the policy is the involvement of pastoral staff as well as the G&T coordinator in any home–school liaison.

The need/problem

T, a very able Year 7 student, is not being stretched in a number of subjects but mathematics has been identified as a particular issue by her parents. The mathematics department does not appear to be catering sufficiently well for this exceptionally able pupil but, with the help of the parents, the department begins to address T's needs, and improves home–school links more generally as a result.

The story

Soon after joining the school in Year 7, it was very clear that T was very able and was showing ability across all subjects, particularly mathematics. T was well-behaved, considerate and task focused. She did not seem unhappy with what was happening in the lessons and had good relationships with nearly all of her peers. In the mathematics lesson, she would often help others who were struggling. Her exercise books were excellently presented and homework was always done to the highest standard. In fact, by the end of the autumn term T seemed to have settled well and was apparently making good progress.

Just before the end of the first term, T's parents contacted the school and asked if they could talk to her form tutor P who was also not a member of the mathematics department. It was initially quite a shock when T's parents declared at the start of the meeting that they were very unhappy. They felt that T had made no progress in the first term and had simply been treading water. They said that they had arranged for T's IQ to be measured and that she was 'gifted' in mathematics. They were particularly concerned because she was 'doing things in the lessons that she had been doing when she was seven'. P spent some time explaining that pupils needed some time to adapt to new surroundings and that pupils were taught in mixed ability groups in Year 7 before being placed into sets at the end of the year. On current performance, T would almost certainly be in the top set but clearly, there was an immediate problem that needed to be resolved.

P thanked the parents for coming in and said that she was pleased they had made contact and she would speak to relevant staff and talk to them again within a couple of weeks but that they should contact her before then if they were worried about anything. P also said that she would wish to speak to T to see how she was feeling and that if one of the parents wished to join her at that time they were welcome, although they declined.

There were an enormous number of issues for P to consider, not least why T might not have had the best from the school. Her first port of call was the mathematics department with a mention to the G&T coordinator about the parents' concerns.

Discussions with the maths department revealed:

- the department were aware of T's particular talents and had spoken to her teacher in the primary school who said that she was working at well above the expectations for her age in most areas

- T had been offered some extension work but had declined

- she was a particular cause for concern because she seemed happy to move along with everyone else and there was no one else in her teaching group they felt she could work with at the same level

- the mathematics department had extension material for nearly all topics but T did what she had to and it was difficult to draw her into anything else.

Discussions with T revealed:

- T did not want to stand out from the crowd

- she was enjoying school and being with her new friends

- she knew her parents were a little concerned that she was not doing lots of homework but she thought they were happy that she seemed happy

- she wouldn't mind doing some new and different things but would prefer to have someone to work with.

P felt that the main issue was probably one of communication and arranged that the mathematics department, G&T coordinator, T and her parents should meet to talk it all through and decide the best next steps.

A series of meetings happened over the year and steadily, with help from a sixth form mentor and some additional support T began to feel sufficiently confident amongst her peers to begin to undertake some of the more challenging work that was available. T was given an IEP (individual education plan) which encouraged communication between the school and T's parents, and the parents were encouraged to contact the school if they had any further concerns. In fact, at the end of Year 7, T moved straight into Year 9 with some preparatory work in several subjects to bridge any potential gaps. T was put into the top set for mathematics.

Commentary including outcomes and next steps

Whilst T was happy with her school experience, she was not being challenged. The school's very flexible and welcoming policy with regard to meeting and discussing issues with parents was clearly very valuable as it raised an issue which needed addressing.

The mathematics department and G&T coordinator took on board the issues of communication and began to work on a strategy for informing parents of able pupils of what was available and how they could best support and encourage their children.

The parents were pleased with the school and its willingness to listen to them and to work together on ensuring that T was challenged whilst remaining enthusiastic about the subject.

In their guide to good practice for home–school liaison (see reference below) the NAGC list the following key points for the school:

- Parents are made to feel welcome in school.

- If parents have concerns about their children, it is clear who they can approach to discuss the situation.

- Parents feel listened to and their concerns are taken seriously.

- The knowledge parents have of their children is valued.

- Possible strategies are discussed with parents before being implemented.

- Parents feel involved in decisions about their children.

The school could also point T and her parents to other sources of help and support for her mathematics, including the NRICH website and YG&T, which would particularly support T in meeting young people with similar interests in academic subjects. T might also consider taking the UKMT mathematics challenges, which may lead to her becoming involved in the Mathematical Olympiads, organised by the BMOC.

Support material

An example of an individual education plan can be found on the website.

Guidance

See case study 11 for another example where an IEP was useful. Some criteria for a good IEP are also offered there.

The following organisations can also provide guidance and support:

- NAGC Development Project: Positive Home–School Liaison, NAGC – The National Association for Gifted Children

- YG&T – http://ygt.dfes.gov.uk

- NRICH – www.nrich.maths.org

- UKMT – www.mathcomp.leeds.ac.uk

- BMOC – www.bmoc.maths.org.

Case study 7 – underachieving mathematicians

Context

School H is a large, seven-form entry undersubscribed 11–16 city comprehensive school, drawing pupils from a small geographic area covering a broad social and ethnic mix. Parental involvement and support is not common, with some notable exceptions from particular ethnic groupings. Maths GCSE results, although improving gradually, are still below national average and the number of A and A* grades is disappointing. Years 7 and 8 are taught in seven mixed ability classes whilst Year 9 upwards is ability set. Half of the ten full-time maths staff have maths or maths related degrees.

The situation

GCSE maths results are not as good as they should be. The staff have been concentrating on raising the number of A–C passes but feel that they have not really been affecting the top sets, which they feel could do better. Both of these conclusions were confirmed by the recent inspection, which also stated that the most able pupils were not being offered a sufficiently challenging mathematical experience and relied too heavily on the teachers for feedback and affirmation.

The story

LA and school targets had been focused around raising the number of A–C grades, with an emphasis on those pupils at the C/D boundary. Most extracurricular activities such as lunchtime sessions and the after-school maths club had been remedial or concentrating on consolidating knowledge and skills. Written in response to the inspection report, the revised school development plan included identifying and monitoring the maths G&T cohort and supporting the maths department through CPD which would help them to plan for offering increased challenge to pupils. At a departmental meeting the curriculum director C suggested that part of the department's CPD budget could be used to buy in specialist advice on underachievement, or increasing challenge in maths, or both.

Working with an external consultant, the department collectively decided that in the top sets in Years 9, 10 and 11 teachers H, K and L would try two strategies for a term, and monitor and evaluate their success. The first strategy was to focus on independent learning – in particularly requiring the students to keep a learning journal (to be shared with their teacher). In this they were to make brief notes at the end of each lesson and describe what topics or aspects they had found easy and what difficult, and use these to plan their own short-term targets. In addition the teachers were going to try to make sure there was some time during each week when as a class they would talk about the way in which they were learning maths. This would be an opportunity for the teachers to emphasise method over result and encourage discussion of targets which were more than the acquisition of facts.

Commentary including outcomes and next steps

Whilst achieving pupils are easy to spot because they produce evidence of their achievement, it is more difficult to spot underachievers and often identification is done firstly on a hunch, backed up by professional experience.

Early researchers (Raph, Goldberg and Passow, 1966) and some recent authors (Davis and Rimm, 1989) have defined underachievement in terms of a gap between ability and expected attainment – a circular argument which is not very helpful. It may be more useful to think about underachievement in three different ways:

- as a behaviour which can change over time. The common description of underachievement as a problem of attitude or work habits is unhelpful because attitudes are more difficult to modify than behaviour. Thus, referring to 'underachieving behaviours' is more helpful when planning a strategy to address the problem.

- underachievement is content- and situation-specific. Gifted children who do not succeed in school are often successful in outside activities such as sports, social occasions and after-school jobs. It is therefore better to label a pupil's behaviour as underachieving in a particular curriculum area rather than label the pupil as an 'underachiever'.

- underachievement is different for different people. A grade C for some (even though they are capable of a higher grade) is acceptable and sufficient whilst for others scraping an A* might be seen as underachieving.

The story continued

The strategies that H, K and L tried in their classes have been written about formally by Whitmore (1980) who describes three types of strategies that she found effective in working with underachieving behaviours in students:

- **supportive strategies**: giving pupils independence and choice can often change the way they perceive the curriculum area. This can be by giving choice from a menu of tasks, or the order or timing of a group of tasks, or perhaps by allowing the pupils to feel they have some say in the way the lesson is organised, as the teachers did above. Able students in particular enjoy feeling in control of their own learning (Naisbett, 2003a).

- **intrinsic strategies**: these strategies incorporate the idea that students' self-concepts as learners are tied closely to their desire to achieve academically. A classroom that encourages positive attitudes through acknowledging innovative or careful methods, rather than only successful answers, is likely to encourage achievement. Supporting pupils in assessing and evaluating their own work is part of this too and this was the main purpose of the diaries, in addition to providing the teachers with feedback.

- **remedial strategies**: with remedial strategies, pupils' strengths are celebrated and weaknesses supported. Highly able pupils' strengths often lead to weaknesses, for example:

  - the ability to see many aspects of a problem may lead to indecision

  - a high activity level may lead to a tendency to rush into things and a lack of concentration

  - greater knowledge of basic facts may lead to a lack of concentration or careless errors.

The diaries helped the pupils to acknowledge their own weaknesses and to seek support.

The strategies H, K and L introduced were not entirely successful to begin with and in faculty discussions they complained that they had not realised how long this would take out of lesson time. However, they decided to stick with them and gradually noticed over the following term that the commentary that the pupils were writing became more automatic and less self-conscious as well as more concise and focused. Through the diaries, the teachers were coming to a greater understanding about the pupils' perceptions of the lessons and they felt that this in turn was having a positive effect on the pupils' behaviour. Class test results were only slightly improved in some cases but even though the quantitative results were not significantly better, the teachers felt that they needed to embed these ideas for a while longer before changing or replacing them.

The next plans were to increase challenge by offering more open-ended activities and investigations. The teachers felt that this would be more successful as a classroom strategy following on from the attempt to increase independence. They introduced this gradually in term three (so this did not affect Year 11) and found it had limited success but the pupils did record enjoying those lessons more than the others. The school is hoping that the GCSE results this year will have improved at the top end and are confident that there will be some change if only small.

Guidance

Montgomery, D. (2000) *Able Underachievers* is a useful reference text.

Case study 8 – bullying

Context

School E is an 11–16 inner city comprehensive with an excellent reputation in the local ethnically and socially diverse community. It involves parents in many of its decision-making processes and encourages them into the school for concerts and subject sessions as well as academic and more general social activities. Parental support is generally positive. The school has an anti-bullying policy which is discussed with pupils in personal and social education sessions, and sent to all parents of new pupils starting at the school. The policy includes details of how to report bullying as a victim or as a witness and the action the school will take. The school regularly reminds pupils of their role in preventing bullying.

The need/problem

A is a very able student. She does not excel in every subject but is certainly the best mathematician and musician in her year group. A has always liked school and enjoys it when her friends ask her for help with their maths and appreciates their patience when she in turn struggles on the netball court. She is certainly not the worst netball player in the year but some of her friends excel at sport in the way she seems to in maths. Her mum describes her friendship group as 'the whole being greater than the sum of the parts' and A thinks this is a very good way to put it. A has always been keen to get to school and meet up with her friends.

The story

A had not been feeling well for a few days; she said she was feeling sick each morning. Her parents were getting a little anxious but on Thursday A said she was feeling better and went to school as usual. She kept very much to herself and when her best friend asked what was wrong A said nothing was wrong and that she just wanted to be left on her own. For the next few weeks A often said she was feeling unwell and not able to go to school but on most days some gentle persuasion at home got her on the bus and into school. However, her parents were feeling a bit concerned and were beginning to discuss the need for a trip to the doctor.

At school A's maths teacher was getting worried: A was very quiet in the lessons, not her usual chirpy self, and had begun to sit on her own. He had seen her arguing with her best friend, which was most unlike her. He recognised some of these symptoms as potentially being linked to bullying, so he informed A's form tutor Mr R who set wheels in motion. Mr R had a quick word with some of A's best friends who said that when she came back from being off sick A had started to act really strangely and did not want to be friends anymore. They had asked A why but A just said she wanted to be on her own. A's friends suspected that something had happened while she was away that had upset her and that it might be to do with a group of pupils that sometimes teased A and who often sniggered at her in PE and called her names. Even if this was not the cause of A's current change of character it was enough to set alarm bells ringing and Mr R informed the head of year.

The existence of the school's anti-bullying policy made what followed easy in the sense that there were clear procedures concerning interviews with pupils, the involvement of parents and other teachers and support for A and the two people who were bullying her. The school also followed up a few months later with further work on trying to ensure that pupils reported concerns as soon as possible as it was felt that A and her friends may have spoken to someone about their concerns if they had felt more confident about the system.

A soon settled back into school but regular reviews were offered to A, with her parents encouraged to let the school know if they were worried. The parents were delighted with the school's response and felt that they had also not taken sufficient notice of the policy. They suggested to the school that parents should be reminded of particular policies as part of the regular communications the school has with homes.

Commentary including outcomes and next steps

Although the policy did not result in pupils or parents acting on concerns at a very early stage it did support the school in acting quickly and effectively in dealing with a particular incident. This illustrates that policies on their own do not change the world but it is how they are used and implemented that is important. There is a wealth of literature available concerning the setting up of policies and how to deal with victims and bullies and some suggested links are given in the guidance below.

Guidance

The following organisations can offer personal help:

- Pupiline – www.pupiline.net

- Childline – www.childline.org.

Case study 9 – dual exceptionality

Context

School G is a selective 11–18 boys' grammar school, drawing its 800+ pupils from a small geographic area in the south of England. Maths GCSE and A level results are excellent and in the top 10% nationally. Boys have to achieve an A at GCSE in order to study A level maths, and in the sixth form of approximately 250, over 50% of boys study single maths with a considerable number studying further maths too. The department has eight full-time staff and a number of part-time staff, and all have a mathematics or mathematics-related degree. In the school there are two pupils with statements of special needs, one of whom has auditory impairment. There is no gifted and talented coordinator since it is assumed that all the pupils are gifted by virtue of gaining entry to the school.

The situation

A discussion prompted by a new colleague together with the arrival at school of a disruptive Year 7 pupil led to a re-examination of the incidence of dyslexia (Specific Learning Difficulties, SpLD) in a highly successful school, with surprising results.

The story

A new member of the maths staff arrived at the school, having previously taught in a large comprehensive in which 15% of the pupils were identified as having special needs. During a whole-school INSET session at the beginning of the new year he expressed surprise that so few pupils were so identified in this school and asked why. The discussion was taken back into the maths department and resulted in an interesting, and at times heated, debate.

The new colleague, F, had read fairly widely on the topic of specific learning difficulties and wondered why in such a large school there were only two pupils who were identified as in need of additional support when dyslexia, for example, is understood to be spread evenly across the population including those who are extremely able. In a school such as this, he stated that it would be expected that at least 50 pupils would be identified with some sort of learning disability. Another colleague, G, claimed that in order to enter the school in the first place, all pupils had had to pass maths, English and verbal reasoning so of course there would not be any special needs pupils in the school. Also since the lowest grade achieved by any pupil in GCSE was a C, and at A level the majority obtained an A or B, no extra support was necessary and he suggested 'if it ain't broke, don't fix it'.

The head of department, M, suggested that the whole department might benefit from finding out more about the whole topic as no-one in the school had any specific expertise. The local educational psychologist was invited in to talk to the maths staff and since her visit was a fairly rare occurrence, colleagues from other departments were invited too and several took up the invitation.

The educational psychologist gave a brief overview of dyslexia – how there are various theories about what it is thought to be, how it might be identified and why a school such as this should be interested in it. After some discussion it was acknowledged that the staff had not really considered that there might be any serious problems with SpLD within their classes, but that on reflection and now that they knew a little more about it, there were pupils who perhaps showed some indications of mild dyslexia. In particular M drew attention to a bright Year 7 pupil, B, who was being disruptive already. Asked to describe his abilities and behaviour, she commented that he was very able orally and frequently offered interesting questions or innovative answers, but his written work was poor and it was when he was required to record that his behaviour began to deteriorate. The presentation of his homework was not of the expected standard either although his work was accurate.

The educational psychologist described several tests that were available to aid diagnosis, some only administered by educational psychologists (e.g. WISC), whilst others could be given by teachers themselves. After discussion it was decided (reluctantly by some colleagues) to start raising the profile by offering a questionnaire to any Year 7 pupils who wanted to take it, in order to see what came out of it. This was done using the questionnaire 'I think I might be dyslexic' available on the Dyslexia Association website (www.bdadyslexia.org.uk). The questionnaire was introduced to the pupils in an informal way and administered at the end of a maths lesson. Several pupils gave interesting results, including B, and it was decided to offer those pupils the Dyslexia Screening Test. A letter was sent home to the pupils' parents and all except one were happy for their child to take the test. The educational psychologist put M in touch with the SENCO from a local school who had experience in administering the test and who was happy to share his expertise with both the school's own SENCO and M. B's results indicated that he might well benefit from extra support and this information was shared with B and his parents. Together the colleagues created an individual education plan (IEP) for B, setting out the steps which the school would take to provide appropriate support, which took the form of a weekly one-to-one hour session with the SENCO, and extra time for assessments in the first instance.

Commentary including outcomes and next steps

There are other SpLD such as dyspraxia (non-verbal, i.e. motor control difficulties), dysorthographia (spelling), dysgraphia (handwriting and fine motor control), attention deficit disorder and dyscalculia (mathematical). Here we have focused on dyslexia but for more information on the others see Montgomery (2003).

Dyslexia, as far as it is possible to tell, is spread evenly across the population and so can be found in pupils of high ability as well as those with low ability although some definitions exclude those who are of very low ability (Gibbs, 1998 and Dyslexia Institute, 1996 in Al-Hroub, 2004). Estimates vary between 4% and 10% of the population. That means that even in highly selective schools there will be a significant number of pupils with dyslexia. Montgomery (2003) suggests that 10% of those with dyslexia are also gifted, i.e. dually exceptional. Usually dyslexia is defined as an inability to read and spell. In a test situation a discrepancy between scores on verbal and non-verbal items can be the key whilst a mismatch between ability and attainment observed by teacher, pupil or parent might support the diagnosis. Some pupils do well on the verbal part of the tests but take longer than would be expected and this too can be a sign that further investigation might be useful.

Al-Hroub (2004) identifies three groups of underachieving dually exceptional children:

- those who have been identified as gifted but have some kind of problem at school and are identified as underachieving

- those who have been identified as having learning difficulties but who are not recognised as highly able although they are

- those who do not appear to be either highly able or exhibiting learning difficulties and 'get by' at school without any support either for their high ability or their learning difficulty.

B fits neatly into the first group in that his learning difficulty had been unrecognised until school became much more academically challenging. His reaction to not being able to keep up was frustration which often resulted in diversionary tactics and he began to drop behind his peers. But, as with so many of these pupils, it was his behaviour that prompted the investigation, not his lower level of achievement. With one-to-one support B's progress was speedy and his behaviour improved. Other departments in the school took on board the support strategies suggested by the SENCO too.

The screening test which had also been given to other pupils indicated that there were several others in the school who were in the third group – they were achieving well enough and were not perceived as a problem or as exceptional. The maths staff were undecided about what to do about these pupils. This is a problem that occurs in many schools – the dyslexia prevents the giftedness from showing and the giftedness means that the pupils appear to be doing fine. Where pupils are predicted Bs or As they are not seen as in need of support but if, with support, they could gain an A* then they are underachieving. M decided to bite the bullet and ask the SENCO to give some additional small group support. The staff at school were encouraged to do some action research and M thought this topic would be a good one to start with. The initiative is still in the early stages but so far the results are promising.

The SEN Code of Practice (2002) requires schools to provide appropriate support so that all children have the opportunity to benefit from an inclusive education. If the SMT had been unwilling to provide resources for B and the other pupils, M could have sought support from the educational psychologist, who could have administered a WISC test and begun the process of applying for a statement of special educational need. If a pupil has such a statement then the LA must provide support as long as that pupil is in the school sector. This does not apply to the sixth form although many schools do continue with support. The funding methodology of sixth forms and sixth form colleges means that they can claim back learning support costs provided they spend £500 (currently) more than they would otherwise on that pupil.

The British Dyslexia Association (BDA) recognises dyslexia friendly local authorities (LAs) with its quality mark scheme. LAs who meet the mark are those who satisfactorily meet the needs of dyslexic learners and fulfil statutory requirements in the LA and in schools. At least 20% of schools within the LA should be dyslexia friendly and it should promote good practice within the LA and in its schools.

Support material

A document *Hints for classroom teachers – dyslexia* is available on the website.

Guidance

The following organisations offer support and guidance:

- British Dyslexia Association – www.bdadyslexia.org.uk

- Dyslexia Action –www.dyslexiaaction.org.uk

- Dyslexia Teachers – www.dyslexia-teacher.com

- National Association for Able Children (NAGC) – www.nagcbritain.org.uk.

Modules for teachers of primary and middle schools can be found at www.standards.dfes.gov.uk/primary/publications/inclusion/1170961/pns_incl1184-2005dyslexia_s4.pdf. The SEN Code of Practice is available from www.teachernet.gov.uk/teachinginengland/detail.cfm?id=390.

Case study 10 – Asperger syndrome

Context

School H is a small, 11–16 rural comprehensive school, drawing pupils from a wide geographic area. In Years 7 to 9, there are three classes, each class having approximately 28 pupils. Year 7 is taught in mixed ability classes whilst Years 8–11 are set. In Years 10 and 11 there are four classes with set four having 15 pupils. The number of pupils on the special needs register is higher than average and the school has a reputation for being very supportive of such pupils.

The situation

A new pupil, Q, joined the top set in Year 8 in January. He arrived with a statement of special educational needs as he had been diagnosed with Asperger syndrome. The teacher was unsure about how to cope with his idiosyncratic behaviour and how to manage it in the class whilst ensuring an appropriate mathematical curriculum for him.

The story

Until Q arrived the class had been working well and the teacher, P, had been pleased with the way that the pupils had taken on board the idea of thinking like mathematicians. Because the class was small (24), P had felt able to try some more risky strategies and had taught several topics through a problem solving approach. The pupils frequently worked in groups and although there were one or two who were more able than the others, on the whole they were a reasonably homogeneous class. Q was obviously very able in maths and particularly in number work where calculations were necessary. He found relating to other people difficult in that he seemed to have little sense of how to behave in a group situation, offered inappropriate remarks and became very agitated towards the end of a lesson when he was required to finish working. P was becoming increasingly concerned that the ethos he had built up in the class was going to be jeopardised by Q's interventions.

P sought guidance from the SENCO and read to inform his own understanding of the syndrome, particularly in a mathematical context. It was clear that Q was a highly functioning Asperger pupil and as such was capable of taking part in planning his own IEP. It was also clear that independent work was not going to be a problem for Q who would probably enjoy carefully chosen projects with clear conclusions whilst group work was going to be difficult and would need careful organisation, perhaps with specific roles for Q and careful choice of sympathetic group members. Together the SENCO, P and Q put together a set of statements that they thought would help other pupils to understand why Q behaved as he sometimes did.

Q enjoyed activities and investigations using the computers, but because he was frequently focused on detail he needed additional support from P in problems which required him to generalise. Over time, P put together a collection of such activities which could be used independently by Q (and those other pupils for whom they were appropriate) and tried to ensure that he gave some individual time to him whilst he was so engaged, in order to support his understanding of generalising.

Because visualising was more difficult for Q than for many of the other pupils, P also requested a copy of a dynamic geometry package for his classroom, primarily for Q. An unexpected consequence was that because he was so focused, Q became the class expert in this and, with guidance from P, devised some activities to support the class in geometric understanding.

Commentary including outcomes and next steps

> Whilst it is true that people with Asperger syndrome have difficulties socialising, and this can be disabling, one does not need to focus on what they cannot do so well – one could instead focus on what they can do well, and perhaps even better than others. Generally, they have normal or above average IQ, can be very accurate at perceiving small details, and may be fascinated by systems and the way things work. These are all qualities that are real advantages in some areas of life.
>
> (Baron-Cohen, 2004)

> Asperger syndrome is frequently linked with giftedness. It is said to be a form of 'autism', but there is no total medical agreement on what is meant by autism or what causes it. Terms such as 'autistic tendencies' or 'autistic spectrum disorder' are sometimes used to imply a range of behaviours from very mild to very severe. There are some remarkable examples of individuals who have extraordinary specific abilities (drawing, memory, calculating) while being extremely limited in all others.
>
> (Lawson *et al.*, 2004)

Psychologist Simon Baron-Cohen and his colleagues at Cambridge's Autism Research Centre have created the Autism-Spectrum Quotient, or AQ, as a measure of the extent of autistic traits in adults. The test looks at the relative strengths of systemising and empathising skills within an individual. A high AQ is one where systemising is high whilst empathising is low, and Baron-Cohen's research indicates that these characteristics also correlate with high mathematical ability.

People with Asperger syndrome have problems in three main areas. These areas are:

- social communication – knowing what to say to other people and understanding what others are saying. Pupils with Asperger take meanings literally and so find puns and some everyday sayings difficult to understand especially as they also find it difficult to read social gestures although they can learn these given time and opportunity. In the classroom situation this means that the teacher needs to be aware of the literal meanings of any communication and throw-away lines meant in jest.

- social understanding – knowing what to do when they are with other people. Many Asperger syndrome pupils have problems with social relationships because they do not understand social rules and may therefore say or do things which of themselves are understandable but inappropriate – they often 'tell it like it is'. In the classroom this means that the teacher has to manage group work carefully and ensure that the group shares an understanding about comments that may be unintentionally rude.

- imagination – Asperger pupils often have passion for some particular aspect of maths which makes them very confident and competent in that area, but they also often find it difficult to switch off or to change from one activity to another quickly. The teacher can minimise this tension by setting out in advance the structure of the lesson and where there may be changes. They may find it difficult to indulge in fantasy or to imagine a scenario, so using visual imagery as a teaching and learning technique may not be helpful for them.

Support material

A document *Teaching pupils with Asperger syndrome* is available on the website.

Guidance

National Autistic Society (www.nas.org.uk) has information and links for teachers, parents and pupils.

Autism, Math, Engineering & the Computer Industry (www.neurodiversity. com/computer_industry.html) is a portal to lots of articles linking maths and autism.

A self-help website including questionnaires can be found at www.gyxe.com/autism/6-047-aspergers-read.shtml.

Case study 11 – exceptionally able

Context

School F is a middle school in a semi-rural location on the edge of a town. Their experience of exceptionally able pupils is very limited but they are keen to offer the best provision for every child and would say that in this respect an exceptionally able child is no different to any other child in that they have a responsibility to offer the best provision possible.

The need/problem

D was a very bright 12-year-old approaching the end of Year 7 who excelled in mathematics and who, since arriving at the school with knowledge and skills well in advance of those of his peers, had been accelerated within his class within normal lesson time. Up to this point, the provision offered by the school had been very successful with the expectation that D would attain very highly in his early entry to Key Stage 3 SATs. However, it was now felt that he required some more individualised provision in order to meet his very special needs. An initial meeting with D and his family indicated a desire that he should be accelerated and take his GCSE early, probably at the end of Year 9. This was not something the school had done before or wished to encourage, except in exceptional circumstances, but they all agreed that D was exceptional. The meeting ended with a decision to offer D a personal mentor from within the staff of the school who would set up an individual education plan (IEP) with D which would identify and set up the next steps. The school agreed to look at early entry with the local upper school and keep D's parents informed using an IEP for D and some follow-up meetings.

The story

D's needs were very special and the school realised that it needed some specialist help. D's mentor arranged for a member of the mathematics department from the local upper school to come to meet D and help with the planning of future provision. In preparation, D was asked to think about what he liked about mathematics and what he would most like to do. D and his mentor started to work on an IEP to help D to monitor his progress against targets, to keep his parents informed and to identify D's long-term aims.

After discussion with a teacher from the upper school, the timetables across the two schools were examined to see if D could attend some of the GCSE sessions there, but this was not possible. Instead, copies of schemes of work and textbooks were lent to the middle school and, as part of their linked community work, it was arranged that a mathematics teacher from the upper school would come down once a week to work with D, using the IEP as a key element in the communication between colleagues.

The IEP was used to identify long-term, medium-term and short-term goals and for D to assess his progress and to get feedback from staff. Long-term plans looked forward over the next two years with targets including taking GCSE early, identifying additional provision and joining NAGTY. Medium-term plans included specific mathematical content to be covered, going to some masterclasses and public lectures, and the use of support through particular online forums. Short-term plans included specific mathematics to cover each week and what D's immediate needs were, for example some extra help with a particular topic or fitting the mathematics into his generally busy schedule. D completed a short personal review at the end of every lesson (what he had done and how he had found it) and a weekly review. Once a fortnight he met with his school mentor to check on progress, but his mathematics teacher also worked with D whenever possible in normal lesson times. By involving staff from the upper school they were also able to prepare for D when he arrived in Year 9.

Commentary including outcomes and next steps

One of the most important aspects of this case study is the long-term planning for the needs of D. It is not enough to identify an individual and then offer unconnected enrichment activities to them. It is important to consider the bigger picture and the long-term development of the individual. In this study a clear long-term aim was identified, but it would have been better to look even further ahead: what is D hoping to do post-GCSE? Has he any long-term plans and ambitions? The IEP is normally associated with pupils with learning difficulties; however it was an invaluable tool in supporting someone who was very able and motivated. It formed a major part of this provision, acting as a guide for D but also as a form of communication with parents and between staff involved in his provision.

Once the system was underway and working well, the middle school could have considered some peer support from either the sixth form in the upper school or undergraduates from one of the local universities as part of their community work.

The upper school needed to start planning for D's arrival and identify ways in which they could offer seamless support. Other potential sources of help included the use of outside mentors, including those from local businesses, or parents.

Towards the end of the year, D went to the upper school to work with his teacher so that he felt comfortable there and that they were aware of what he was doing. He managed to join in with one or two of the Year 10 lessons, anticipating that he might be able to take some of his lessons with them in the following year.

Guidance

Individual education plans should:

- be simple to use

- be working documents

- give detailed information on the provision being offered

- list achievable short- and long-term targets and support planning

- cover the needs of all staff involved and parents

- be accessible

- help with effective planning

- help pupils monitor their own progress

- result in the achievement of learning goals

- identify clear targets for learning including long-, medium- and short-term targets set for, by or with the pupil

- identify the resource implications including teaching allocation and other support

- give clear timescales for meeting targets and regular review

- list success criteria and outcomes.

Support material

An example of an individual education plan can be found on the website.

The DfES/QCA publication *A Condensed Key Stage 3: Designing a Flexible Curriculum* (2004) may also be of use.

Appendices

Institutional quality standards in gifted and talented education

Generic Elements	Entry	Developing	Exemplary
		A – Effective teaching and learning strategies	
1. Identification	i. The school/college has learning conditions and systems to identify gifted and talented pupils in all year groups and an agreed definition and shared understanding of the meaning of 'gifted and talented' within its own, local and national contexts.	i. Individual pupils are screened annually against clear criteria at school/college and subject/topic level.	i. **Multiple criteria and sources of evidence** are used to identify gifts and talents, including through the use of a broad range of quantitative and qualitative data.
	ii. An **accurate record** of the identified gifted and talented population is kept and updated.	ii. The record is used to identify under-achievement and **exceptional achievement** (both within and outside the population) and to track/review pupil **progress**.	ii. The record is supported by a comprehensive monitoring, progress planning and reporting system which all staff regularly share and contribute to.
	iii. The identified gifted and talented population broadly reflects the school/college's **social and economic composition**, gender and ethnicity.	iii. **Identification** systems address issues of **multiple exceptionality** (pupils with specific gifts/talents and special educational needs).	iii. Identification processes are regularly reviewed and refreshed in the light of pupil performance and value-added data. The gifted and talented population is fully representative of the school/college's population.
Evidence			
Next steps			
2. Effective provision in the classroom	i. The school/college addresses the different needs of the gifted and talented population by providing a stimulating learning environment and by extending the teaching repertoire.	i. Teaching and learning strategies are diverse and flexible, meeting the needs of distinct pupil groups within the gifted and talented population (e.g. able underachievers, exceptionally able).	i. The school/college has established a range of methods to find out what works best in the classroom, and shares this within the school/college and with other schools and colleges.
	ii. Teaching and learning is differentiated and delivered through both individual and group activities.	ii. A range of challenging learning and teaching strategies is evident in lesson planning and delivery. **Independent learning** skills are developed.	ii. Teaching and learning are suitably challenging and varied, incorporating the breadth, depth and pace required to progress high achievement. Pupils routinely work independently and self-reliantly.

	Level 1	Level 2	Level 3
	iii. Opportunities exist to extend learning through **new technologies.**	iii. The use of **new technologies** across the curriculum is focused on **personalised learning** needs.	iii. The innovative use of new technologies raises the achievement and motivation of gifted and talented pupils.
Evidence			
Next steps			
3. Standards	i. Levels of **attainment** and **achievement** for gifted and talented pupils are comparatively high in relation to the rest of the school/college population and are in line with those of similar pupils in similar schools/colleges.	i. Levels of **attainment** and **achievement** for gifted and talented pupils are broadly consistent across the gifted and talented population and above those of similar pupils in similar schools/colleges.	i. Levels of attainment and achievement for gifted and talented pupils indicate sustainability over time and are well above those of similar pupils in similar schools/colleges.
	ii. Self-evaluation indicates that gifted and talented provision is satisfactory.	ii. Self-evaluation indicates that gifted and talented provision is good.	ii. Self-evaluation indicates that gifted and talented provision is very good or excellent.
	iii. Schools/colleges' gifted and talented education programmes are explicitly linked to the achievement of SMART outcomes and these highlight improvements in pupils' attainment and achievement.		
Evidence			
Next steps			

B – Enabling curriculum entitlement and choice

	Level 1	Level 2	Level 3
4. Enabling curriculum entitlement and choice	i. Curriculum organisation is flexible, with opportunities for enrichment and increasing subject/topic choice. Pupils are provided with support and guidance in making choices.	i. The curriculum offers opportunities and guidance to pupils which enable them to work beyond their age and/or phase, and across subjects or topics, according to their aptitudes and interests.	i. The curriculum offers personalised learning pathways for pupils which maximise individual potential, retain flexibility of future choices, extend well beyond test/examination requirements and result in sustained impact on pupil attainment and achievement.
Evidence			
Next steps			

Definitions for words and phrases in bold are provided in the glossary in the Quality Standards *User Guide*, available at www2.teachernet.gov.uk/gat. QS Model October 2005

© Crown Copyright 2005–2007.

Generic Elements	Entry	Developing	Exemplary
C – Assessment for learning			
5. Assessment for learning	i. Processes of data analysis and pupil assessment are employed throughout the school/college to plan learning for gifted and talented pupils. ii. Dialogue with pupils provides focused feedback which is used to plan future learning. iii. Self and peer assessment, based on clear understanding of criteria, are used to increase pupils' responsibility for learning.	i. Routine progress reviews, using both qualitative and quantitative data, make effective use of prior, predictive and value-added attainment data to plan for progression in pupils' learning. ii. Systematic oral and written feedback helps pupils to set challenging curricular targets. iii. Pupils reflect on their own skill development and are involved in the design of their own targets and tasks.	i. Assessment data are used by teachers and across the school/college to ensure challenge and sustained progression in individual pupils' learning. ii. Formative assessment and individual target setting combine to maximise and celebrate pupils' achievements. iii. Classroom practice regularly requires pupils to reflect on their own progress against targets, and engage in the direction of their own learning.
Evidence			
Next steps			
6. Transfer and transition	i. Shared processes, using agreed criteria, are in place to ensure the productive transfer of information from one setting to another (i.e. from class to class, year to year and school/college to school/college).	i. Transfer information concerning gifted and talented pupils, including parental input, informs targets for pupils to ensure progress in learning. Particular attention is given to including new admissions.	i. Transfer data concerning gifted and talented pupils are used to inform planning of teaching and learning at subject/aspect/topic and individual pupil level, and to ensure progression according to ability rather than age or phase.
Evidence			
Next steps			
D – School/college organisation			
7. Leadership	i. A named member of the governing body, senior management team and the lead professional responsible for gifted and talented education have clearly directed responsibilities for motivating and driving gifted and talented provision. The head teacher actively champions gifted and talented provision.	i. Responsibility for gifted and talented provision is distributed, and evaluation of its impact shared, at all levels in the school/college. Staff subscribe to policy at all levels. Governors play a significant supportive and evaluative role.	i. Organisational structures, communication channels and the deployment of staff (e.g. workforce remodelling) are flexible and creative in supporting the delivery of personalised learning. Governors take a lead in celebrating achievements of gifted and talented pupils.
Evidence			
Next steps			

8. Policy	i. The gifted and talented policy is integral to the school/college's inclusion agenda and approach to personalised learning, feeds into and from the single school/college improvement plan and is consistent with other policies.	i. The policy directs and reflects best practice in the school/college, is regularly reviewed and is clearly linked to other policy documentation.	i. The policy includes input from the whole school/college community and is regularly refreshed in the light of innovative national and international practice.
Evidence			
Next steps			
9. School/college ethos and pastoral care	i. The school/college sets high expectations, recognises achievement and celebrates the successes of all its pupils. ii. The school/college identifies and addresses the particular social and emotional needs of gifted and talented pupils in consultation with pupils, parents and carers.	i. The school/college fosters an environment which promotes positive behaviour for learning. Pupils are listened to and their views taken into account. ii. Strategies exist to counteract bullying and any adverse effects of social and curriculum pressures. Specific support for able underachievers and pupils from different cultures and social backgrounds is available and accessible.	i. An ethos of ambition and achievement is agreed and shared by the whole school/college community. Success across a wide range of abilities is celebrated. ii. The school/college places equal emphasis on high achievement and emotional well being, underpinned by programmes of support personalised to the needs of gifted and talented pupils. There are opportunities for pupils to use their gifts to benefit other pupils and the wider community.
Evidence			
Next steps			
10. Staff development	i. Staff have received professional development in meeting the needs of gifted and talented pupils.	i. The induction programme for new staff addresses gifted and talented issues, both at whole school/college and specific subject/aspect level.	i. There is ongoing audit of staff needs and an appropriate range of professional development in gifted and talented education. Professional development is informed by research and collaboration within and beyond the school/college.

Definitions for words and phrases in bold are provided in the glossary in the Quality Standards *User Guide*, available at www2.teachernet.gov.uk/gat. QS Model October 2005

© Crown Copyright 2005–2007.

Generic Elements	Entry	Developing	Exemplary
	ii. The lead professional responsible for gifted and talented education has received appropriate professional development.	ii. Subject/aspect and phase leaders have received specific professional development in meeting the needs of gifted and talented pupils.	ii. Priorities for the development of gifted and talented provision are included within a professional development entitlement for all staff and are monitored through performance management processes.
Evidence			
Next steps			
11. Resources	i. Provision for gifted and talented pupils is supported by appropriate budgets and resources.	i. Allocated resources include school/college based and nationally available resources, and these have a significant and measurable impact on the progress that pupils make and their attitudes to learning.	i. Resources are used to stimulate innovative and experimental practice, which is shared throughout the school/college and which are regularly reviewed for impact and best value.
Evidence			
Next steps			
12. Monitoring and evaluation	i. Subject and phase audits focus on the quality of teaching and learning for gifted and talented pupils. Whole school/college targets are set using prior attainment data.	i. Performance against targets (including at pupil level) is regularly reviewed. Targets include qualitative pastoral and curriculum outcomes as well as numerical data.	i. Performance against targets is rigorously evaluated against clear criteria. Qualitative and quantitative outcomes inform whole-school/college self-evaluation processes.
	ii. Elements of provision are planned against clear objectives within effective whole-school self-evaluation processes.	ii. All elements, including non-academic aspects of gifted and talented provision, are planned to clear objectives and are subjected to detailed evaluation.	ii. The school/college examines and challenges its own provision to inform development of further experimental and innovative practice in collaboration with other schools/colleges.
Evidence			
Next steps			

E – Strong partnerships beyond the school

	Entry	Developing	Exemplary
13. Engaging with the community, families and beyond	i. Parents/carers are aware of the school's/college's policy on gifted and talented provision, contribute to its identification processes and are kept informed of developments in gifted and talented provision, including through the School Profile. ii. The school/college shares good practice and has some collaborative provision with other schools, colleges and the wider community.	i. Progression of gifted and talented pupils is enhanced by home-school/college partnerships. There are strategies to engage and support hard-to-reach parents/carers. ii. A coherent strategy for networking with other schools, colleges and local community organisations extends and enriches provision.	i. Parents/carers are actively engaged in extending provision. Support for gifted and talented provision is integrated with other children's services (e.g. Sure Start, EAL, traveller, refugee, LAC Services). ii. There is strong emphasis on collaborative and innovative working with other schools/colleges which impacts on quality of provision locally, regionally and nationally.
Evidence			
Next steps			
14. Learning beyond the classroom	i. There are opportunities for pupils to learn beyond the school/college day and site (extended hours and out-of-school activities). ii. Pupils participate in dedicated gifted and talented activities (e.g. summer schools) and their participation is recorded.	i. A coherent programme of enrichment and extension activities (through extended hours and out-of-school activities) complements teaching and learning and helps identify pupils' latent gifts and talents. ii. Local and national provision helps meet individual pupils' learning needs, e.g. NAGTY membership, accessing outreach, local enrichment programmes.	i. Innovative models of learning beyond the classroom are developed in collaboration with local and national schools/colleges to further enhance teaching and learning. ii. Coherent strategies are used to direct and develop individual expert performance via external agencies, e.g. HE/FE links, online support, and local/regional/national programmes.
Evidence			
Next steps			

Definitions for words and phrases in bold are provided in the glossary in the Quality Standards *User Guide*, available at www2.teachernet.gov.uk/gat. QS Model October 2005

© Crown Copyright 2005–2007.

Basic audit form

Aspect of provision	Commentary	Strengths	Development points	Possible actions

From *Meeting the Needs of Your Most Able Pupils: Mathematics*, Routledge 2007

Detailed audit form

Generic elements	Entry		Developing		Exemplary	
	Ref	✓/✗	Ref	✓/✗	Ref	✓/✗
Identification						
1. Identification	i		i		i	
	ii		ii		ii	
	iii		iii		iii	
Provision						
2. Entitlement and choice	i		i		i	
3. Grouping	i		i		i	
4. In the classroom	i		i		i	
	ii		ii		ii	
	iii		iii		iii	
5. Learning beyond the classroom	i		i		i	
	ii		ii		ii	
Assessment						
6. Standards	i		i		i	
7. Assessment for learning	i		i		i	
	ii		ii		ii	
	iii		iii		iii	
General departmental issues						
8. Ethos and pastoral care	i		i		i	
	ii		ii		ii	
9. Staff	i		i		i	
10. Staff development	i		i		i	
11. Resources	i		i		i	
12. Transfer and transition	i		i		i	
13. Partnerships	i		i		i	
	ii		ii		ii	
Engaging with the community, families and beyond						
14. Monitoring and evaluation	i		i		i	
	ii		ii		ii	
Overall	Entry		Developing		Exemplary	

Departmental monitoring and evaluation guidelines

Generic Elements	Entry	Exemplary
	Identification	
1. Identification	i The department has systems to identify gifted pupils in all year groups and there is a shared understanding of what it is to be 'gifted' in mathematics.	i A range of quantitative and qualitative evidence is used to identify able pupils and their particular strengths and needs.
	ii A record of able pupils is kept and used to inform future provision as well as the whole-school G&T register.	i Individual pupils are screened annually. Parents/carers are involved in the identification process.
		ii The record is supported by a comprehensive monitoring and reporting system which all members of the department contribute to.
	iii The identified gifted cohort broadly reflects the school's social and economic composition, gender and ethnicity.	ii The record is used to identify under-achievement and exceptional achievement (both within and outside the cohort) and to track/review pupil progress. Information is shared with other subject areas and the pastoral team.
		iii Identification systems address issues of dual exceptionality.
		iii Identification processes are regularly reviewed and refreshed in the light of pupil performance and value-added data. Findings are shared with pastoral and subject staff in other areas of the school/college.
	Provision	
2. Entitlement and choice	i Curriculum organisation is flexible, with opportunities for a range of provision. Pupils are provided with support and guidance in making choices.	i Curriculum offers opportunities for acceleration (where appropriate), extension and enrichment activities including cross-subject links. Curriculum strategies take into account long-term sustainability.
		i Curriculum offers personalised learning pathways for pupils which maximise individual potential, retain flexibility of future choices, extend well beyond test/examination requirements and result in sustained impact on pupil attainment and achievement.
3. Grouping	i Grouping strategies are employed that support the diverse needs of all pupils.	i Some flexible grouping strategies are used to support able pupils.
		i Grouping strategies are flexible and respond to individual needs.

4. In the classroom	i The department addresses the different needs of the gifted and talented cohort by providing a stimulating learning environment.		i The department engages in reflective practice, including action research, to improve the learning environment. Colleagues share effective classroom practice with other schools and colleges.
	ii Teaching and learning is differentiated and is delivered through both individual and group activities.		ii Teaching and learning offers the challenge, breadth, depth and pace required to progress high achievement. Personalised learning is integral to in-class provision. Pupils are encouraged to develop independence and self-reliance.
	iii Opportunities exist to extend learning through new technologies.		iii The innovative use of new technologies raises the achievement and motivation of gifted and talented pupils.
5. Learning beyond the classroom	i There are opportunities for pupils to learn and develop beyond normal lesson times.		i The school-based provision is developed alongside external provision to offer an extensive range of opportunities for able pupils.
	ii Pupils participate in extracurricular activities such as masterclasses and summer schools, YG&T membership and online groups.		ii Coherent strategies are used to direct and develop individuals via out of school programmes, including HE links. Pupils' out-of-school activities feed back into the department and affect school-based provision.

Assessment

6. Standards	i Levels of attainment and achievement for gifted pupils are in line with those of similar pupils in similar schools/colleges and in other subject areas.	i Levels of attainment and achievement for gifted pupils are above those of similar pupils in similar schools/colleges and in other subject areas.	i Levels of attainment and achievement (value-added) for gifted pupils are well above those of similar pupils in similar schools/colleges, and indicate sustainability over time.

Generic Elements	Entry		Exemplary
7. Assessment for learning	i	Processes of data analysis and pupil assessment are employed throughout the department to plan for learning.	i Assessment data are used by teachers and across departments to ensure challenge and sustained progression of individual pupils' learning.
	i	Routine progress reviews make use of prior, predictive and value-added attainment data to plan progression of pupil groups.	
	ii	Dialogue with pupils is used to plan for future learning.	ii Formative assessment and individual target setting combine to maximise and celebrate pupil achievement.
	ii	Systematic oral and written feedback helps pupils to set challenging curricular targets.	
	iii	Self- and peer-assessment, based on clear understanding of criteria, are used to increase pupils' responsibility for learning.	iii Classroom practice regularly requires pupils to reflect on their own progress and engage in the direction of their own learning. Teachers and pupils work collaboratively to support individual needs.
	iii	Pupils reflect on their own skill development and are involved in the design of their own targets and tasks, which in turn informs future provision.	

General departmental issues

Generic Elements	Entry		Exemplary
8. Ethos and pastoral care	i	The department sets high expectations, recognises achievement and celebrates the successes of all its pupils.	i An ethos of ambition and achievement is agreed and shared by the pupils, parents and the staff. Success is celebrated.
	i	The department fosters an inclusive view of gifted education in an environment which promotes positive behaviour for learning, where it is good to achieve and pupils' views are valued.	
	ii	The department addresses the particular social and emotional needs of gifted and talented pupils.	ii The department places equal emphasis on high achievement and emotional well-being, underpinned by programmes of support personalised to the needs of gifted pupils. There are opportunities for pupils to use their gifts to benefit other pupils and the wider community.
	ii	Strategies exist to counteract bullying and any adverse effects of social and curriculum pressures. Specific support for able underachievers and pupils from different cultures and social backgrounds is available and accessible.	
9. Staff	i	A named member of staff has responsibility for motivating and driving gifted and talented provision within the department.	i Responsibility for gifted provision is seen as shared by all staff in the department, who are clear about their responsibilities.
	i	Organisational structures and the deployment of staff are flexible and creative in supporting communication channels and the delivery of personalised learning.	

10. Staff development	i	All staff (including support personnel and the member of staff with specific responsibility for gifted provision) have received training in meeting the needs of gifted and talented pupils.	i	The induction programme for new staff addresses gifted issues. CPD provision fully integrates the needs of adults other than teachers and also covers how to make effective use of non-teaching staff for supporting gifted provision. Outcomes from professional development courses are shared with colleagues.	i	Specific needs of staff (including support staff) are identified as part of the review process. CPD provision is included and is informed by action research and collaboration within and beyond the department.
11. Resources	i	Provision for gifted and talented pupils is supported by appropriate budgets and resources.	i	Allocated resources include department based and nationally available resources, and these have a significant and measurable impact on pupils' progress and attitudes.	i	Resources are used to stimulate innovative and experimental practice, which is shared throughout the department and regularly reviewed for impact and best value.
12. Transfer and transition	i	Processes are in place to ensure the productive transfer of information from one setting to another (i.e. from class to class, year to year and department to department).	i	Transfer information, including parental input, informs targets for pupils to ensure progress in learning. Particular attention is given to new admissions.	i	Transfer data are used to inform planning of teaching and learning at aspect/topic and individual pupil level, and to ensure progression according to ability.
13. Partnerships	i	The department shares good practice and makes collaborative provision with other schools, colleges and the wider community.	i	A coherent strategy for networking with mathematics departments in other schools, colleges and local community organisations extends and enriches provision.	i	There is strong emphasis on collaborative working with other schools/colleges to improve practice, and to impact on quality of provision locally, regionally and nationally.
	ii	Progression of gifted pupils is enhanced by home–department partnerships.	ii	There are strategies to engage and support hard-to-reach parents/carers.	ii	Parents/carers are actively engaged in extending provision. Support for gifted and talented provision is integrated with other children's services (EAL, travellers, refugees, LAC) through the school G&T coordinator.

Generic Elements	Entry		Exemplary	
		Monitoring and Evaluation		
14. Monitoring and evaluation	i	Subject audits have been completed and department targets are set using a range of information (including attainment data).	i	Performance against targets is rigorously evaluated against clear criteria. Outcomes inform whole department self-evaluation processes and feed into whole-school evaluation procedure.
	ii	Elements of provision are planned against clear objectives.	ii	Evidence from action research into provision informs development of further experimental and innovative practice, in collaboration with other schools/colleges.

Monitoring and Evaluation

i   Performance against targets (including at pupil level) is regularly reviewed.

ii   All elements of gifted and talented provision are planned to clear objectives and are subjected to detailed evaluation.

From *Meeting the Needs of Your Most Able Pupils: Mathematics*, Routledge 2007

Outline form to support action planning

Policy objective	Specific focus	Targets	Actions	Measurable outcomes	Staff	Resources needed	Completion date	Review date

 From *Meeting the Needs of Your Most Able Pupils: Mathematics*, Routledge 2007

Appendix 2.4

Mathematical ability

Able mathematicians can . . .

- understand the structure of the problem in a way that helps them to know how to begin to solve it

- extract a pattern from a set of examples and generalise it

- generalise approaches to problem solving

- develop chains of reasoning using logic

- leave out steps in an argument

- use mathematical symbols flexibly as an aid to, and as part of, thinking

- think flexibly – change their approach if necessary and switch between different representations or ways of thinking

- start from the answer and work backwards if it seems helpful

- remember generalised relationships, types of problems and types of solutions.

(Krutetskii)

Pupils who are gifted in mathematics are likely to:

- learn and understand mathematical ideas quickly

- work systematically and accurately

- be more analytical; think logically and see mathematical relationships

- make connections between the concepts they have learned; identify patterns easily

- apply their knowledge to new or unfamiliar contexts

- communicate their reasoning and justify their methods

- ask questions that show clear understanding of, and curiosity about, mathematics

- take a creative approach to solving mathematical problems

- sustain their concentration throughout longer tasks and persist in seeking solutions

- be more adept at posing their own questions and pursuing lines of enquiry.

(QCA website)

From *Meeting the Needs of Your Most Able Pupils: Mathematics*, Routledge 2007

Key review questions

- Is there agreement within the department about what constitutes high ability in mathematics?

- Does this accord with the school view?

- Do you consider the whole range of high ability or only those aspects which are easily identified?

- Is there a strong link between the school's identification strategies and those of the mathematics department?

- Within the department, is there a balance between test scores and teacher nomination?

- Is sufficient information provided to your colleagues to support them in identifying able mathematicians?

- Are all colleagues aware of the purpose of identifying able pupils?

- Do you use information from outside the department – parental nomination for example?

- Does your cohort represent the full range of pupils in the school?

- Is there a nominated member of staff responsible for coordinating the identification strategy?

- Is your strategy open to review and change?

(Adapted from Bentley (2003) *Curriculum Briefing*, 1 (2). London: Optimus publishing.)

References

Al-Hroub, A. (2004) *Gifted Children with Learning Difficulties: Definitions, Identification And Characteristics.* Paper presented at BERA 17th September 2004.

Andrews, P. (2002) Angle Measurement: An Opportunity for Equity. *Mathematics in School,* **31** (5). The Mathematical Association.

Baron-Cohen, S. (2003) Empathising and systemising in adults with and without Asperger Syndrome. *Journal of Autism and Developmental Disorder,* **34** (3).

Baron-Cohen, S. (2004) The empathy quotient: an investigation of adults with Asperger syndrome or high functioning autism, and normal sex differences. *Journal of Autism and Developmental Disorder,* **34** (2).

Baron-Cohen, S. (2005) www.autismresearchcentre.com/research/project.asp?id= 102.

Bloom, B. (1956) *A taxonomy of educational objectives: cognitive domain.* New York: Mackay.

Bloom, B. S. (1984) *Taxonomy of educational objectives.* Boston, MA: Allyn and Bacon.

Boaler, J. (1997) *Experiencing School Mathematics.* Buckingham: Open University Press.

Boaler, J., Wiliam, D. *et al.* (2000) Students' experiences of ability grouping – dissatisfaction, polarisation and the construction of failure. *British Educational Research Journal,* **26** (5), 631–48.

Cognitive Ability Tests. www.nfer-nelson.co.uk/cat/cat_faq.asp.

Craven, R. G., Marsh, H. W. *et al.* (2000) Gifted, streamed and mixed-ability programs for gifted students. *Impact on self-concept, motivation, and achievement,* **44** (1), 51–75.

Davis, G. A. and Rimm, S. B. (1989) *Education of the Gifted and Talented,* 2nd edn. Englewood Cliffs, NJ: Prentice-Hall.

Department for Education and Employment and QCA (1999) *Mathematics: The National Curriculum for England and Wales.* London: DfEE and QCA.

Department for Education and Employment (2001) *Key Stage 3 – National Strategy: Framework for Teaching Mathematics: Years 7, 8 and 9.* London: DfEE.

Department for Education and Skills and QCA (2004) *A Condensed Key Stage 3: Designing a Flexible Curriculum.* London: DfES.

Department for Education and Skills (2005a) *Guidance on Identification.* www.standards.dfes.gov.uk/giftedandtalented/guidanceandtraining/roleofcoor dinators/identificationofgt.

Department for Education and Skills (2005b) Module 3 *Guidance on Teaching G and T pupils.* www.standards.dfes.gov.uk/keystage3/respub/agt.

Dracup, T. (2003) Understanding the national approach to gifted and talented students, *Curriculum Briefing,* **1** (2), London: Optimus.

EiC Guidance (2005) www.standards.dfes.gov.uk/my/sie/eic/EiCOverview/News/ SelfPeerReviewCriteria.

Eric digest. www.hoagiesgifted.org/eric/Archived/e478.html.

Eyre, D. (1997) *Able Children in Ordinary Schools*. London: David Fulton Publishers.

Eyre, D. and Fitzpatrick, M. (2000) Able children with additional special needs, in Benton and O'Brien (eds) *Special Needs and the Beginning Teacher*. London: Continuum.

Freeman, J. (2005) *National Coordinators Training Programme*, www.brookes. ac.uk/schools/education/rescon/cpdgifted.

Gardiner, E. A. (2005) *Where Will the Next Generation of UK Mathematicians Come From?* Preliminary report, supported by Manchester Institute for Mathematical Sciences, by the London Mathematical Society, the Institute of Mathematics and Applications and the UK Mathematics Foundation.

Gardner, H. (1993) *Frames of Mind: the Theory of Multiple Intelligences*, 2nd edn. New York: Basic Books.

Geake, J. (1999) *Educating the Very Able – Current International Research with a special slant towards mathematics*, http://nrich.maths.org/public/viewer.php? obj_id=5661.

Geake, J. G. (2003) Young mathematical brains. *Primary Mathematics*, 7 (1), 14–18.

George, W. C., Cohn, S. J. *et al.* (eds) (1979) *Educating the Gifted: Acceleration or Enrichment*. Revised and expanded proceedings of the Ninth Annual Hyman Blumberg Symposium on Research in Early Childhood Education. Baltimore and London: The Johns Hopkins University Press.

Gibbs, G. (1988) *Learning By Doing: A Guide to Teaching and Learning Methods*. Oxford: Further Education Unit, Oxford Polytechnic.

Ireson, J., Hallan, S. *et al.* (2005) What are the effects of ability grouping on GCSE attainment? *British Educational Research Journal*, 31 (4), 443–58.

Kennard, R. (2001) *Teaching Mathematically Able Children*, 2nd edn. London: David Fulton Publishers.

Kerry, T. and Kerry, C. (2000) The centrality of teaching skills in improving able pupil education. *Educating Able Children*, Autumn 2000, 13–19.

Koshy, V. (2004) Nurturing children's mathematical promise. *Maths Coordinator File*, no. 18. London: pfp Electric Word.

Krutetskii, V. A. (1976) J. Teller (trans.) in Kilpatrick, J. and Wirszup, I. (eds) *The Psychology of Mathematical Abilities in School Children*. Chicago: University of Chicago Press.

Lawson, J., Baron-Cohen, S. and Wheelwright, S. (2004) www.autismresearchcentre. com/docs/papers/2004_Lawson_etal_JADD.pdf.

Mason, J., Burton, L. and Stacey, K. (1986) *Thinking Mathematically*. Harlow: Pearson Education Ltd.

Meunier, J. (2003) *Practical Intelligence*, www.indiana.edu/~intell/practical intelligence.shtml.

MidYIS (2005) www.midyisproject.org.

Montgomery, D. (2003) *Gifted and Talented Children with Special Needs Double Exceptionality*. London: Fulton.

Montgomery, D. (2000) *Able Underachievers*. London: Whurr.

NAGTY (2005) Unpublished case studies PGCE+ course. NAGTY: Warwick University.

Naisbett, A. (2003a) 'Able children like. . .' in *National Coordinator Training Materials*. Oxford: Oxford Brookes University.

Naisbett, A. (2003b) *Creating the Inclusive Classroom*. Redcar and Cleveland LEA.

National Primary Trust (1999) *Transition for Gifted and Talented Pupils – The Issues*.

Neiderer, K. and Irwin, K. (2001) *Using Problem Solving to Identify Mathematically Gifted Students*. Paper presented at PME.

Neiderer, K. *et al.* (2003) Identification of mathematically gifted children in New Zealand. *High Ability Studies*, **14** (1).

Ofsted (2002) *Changing Schools: Evaluation of the Effectiveness of Transfer Arrangements at Age 11*. June report from the Office of Her Majesty's Chief Inspector of Schools, HMI 550 Version 21 June 2002 E-publication.

Ofsted (2003a) Excellence in Cities and Education Action Zones: HMI 1399 May 2003.

Ofsted (2003b) *Handbook for Inspecting Secondary Schools*. London: Ofsted. (An HTML version is available at www.ofsted.gov.uk.)

Olkin, I. and Schoenfeld, A. H. (1994) A discussion of Bruce Reznick's chapter [some thoughts on writing for the Putnam] in Schoenfeld, A, H., *Mathematical Thinking and Problem Solving*. Hillside, N.J.: Lawrence Erlbaum. 39–51.

Perks, P. A. (2001) *Adapting and Extending Secondary Maths Activities – New Tasks for Old*. London: David Fulton Publishers.

Piggott, J. (2006) An investigation into the nature of mathematical enrichment: a case study of implementation: Doctoral Thesis, Institute of Education, London.

Piggott, J. and Back, J. (2004) A problem is only a problem when you can't do it. *Primary Mathematics*, Autumn 04. The Mathematical Association.

Polya, G. (1957) *How to Solve it*. Princeton: Princeton University Press.

Prestage, S. and Perks, P. (2001) *Adapting and Extending Secondary Mathematics Activities*. London: Fulton.

Raph, J. B., Goldberg, M. L. and Passow, A. H. (1966) *Bright Underachievers*. New York: Teachers College Press.

Renzulli, J. (2005) *The Three-Ring Conception of Giftedness*, www.sp.uconn.edu/~nrcgt/sem/semart13.html.

Rimm, S. (1986) *The Underachievement Syndrome: Causes And Cures*. Watertown, WI: Apple Publishing Company.

Schoenfeld, A. H. (1985) *Mathematical Problem Solving*. Orlando: Academic Press.

Schoenfeld, A. (ed.) (1994) *Mathematical Thinking and Problem Solving*. Hillsdale, NJ: Lawrence Erlbaum Associates.

Skemp, R. (1971) *The Psychology of Learning Mathematics*. London: Penguin.

Sternberg, R. J. (1985) *Beyond IQ: A Triarchic Theory of Intelligence*. Cambridge: CUP.

Sukhnandan, L. and Lee, B. (1998) *Streaming, Setting and Grouping by Ability: A Review of. the Literature*. Slough: NFER.

Trafton, P. (1981) Overview of providing for mathematically able students. *The arithmetic teacher,* **28** (6), 12–13. Cambridge: CUP.

Watson, A., De Geest, E. *et al.* (2003) *Deep Progress in Mathematics: The Improving Attainment in Mathematics Project.* Oxford: University of Oxford.

Watson, A. and Mason, J. (1998) *Questions and Prompts for Mathematical Thinking.* Derby: Association of Teachers of Mathematics.

Wenger, E., McDermott, R. *et al.* (2002) *A Guide to Managing Knowledge: Cultivating Communities of Practice.* Harvard: Harvard Business School Press.

Whitmore, J. F. (1980) *Giftedness, Conflict and Underachievement.* Boston: Allyn and Bacon.

Winstanley, C. (2005) *Too Clever by Half.* London: Trentham.

World Class Arena (2005) www.worldclassarena.org/v5/default.htm.

YELLIS (2005) www.yellisproject.org.